MY CRAZY IMPERFECT

CHRISTIAN FAMILY

MY CRAZY IMPERFECT CHRISTIAN FAMILY

Living Out Your
Faith with Those
Who Know You Best

GLENN T. STANTON

NAVPRESS®

Bringing Truth to Life

OUR GUARANTEE TO YOU

We believe so strongly in the message of our books that we are making this quality guarantee to you. If for any reason you are disappointed with the content of this book, return the title page to us with your name and address and we will refund to you the list price of the book. To help us serve you better, please briefly describe why you were disappointed. Mail your refund request to: NavPress, P.O. Box 35002, Colorado Springs, CO 80935.

The Navigators is an international Christian organization. Our mission is to reach, disciple, and equip people to know Christ and to make Him known through successive generations. We envision multitudes of diverse people in the United States and every other nation who have a passionate love for Christ, live a lifestyle of sharing Christ's love, and multiply spiritual laborers among those without Christ.

NavPress is the publishing ministry of The Navigators. NavPress publications help believers learn biblical truth and apply what they learn to their lives and ministries. Our mission is to stimulate spiritual formation among our readers.

ISBN 1-57683-403-4

Cover design by Kirk Pounce, UDG/DesignWorks
Cover photo by Lisa Pines, Photonica
Creative Team: Toben Heim, Brad Lewis, Pat Miller

Some of the anecdotal illustrations in this book are true to life and are included with the permission of the persons involved. All other illustrations are composites of real situations, and any resemblance to people living or dead is coincidental.

Unless otherwise identified, all Scripture quotations in this publication are taken from the *New American Standard Bible* (NASB), © The Lockman Foundation 1960, 1962, 1963, 1968, 1971, 1972, 1973, 1975, 1977. Other versions used include the HOLY BIBLE: NEW INTERNATIONAL VERSION® (NIV®), Copyright © 1973, 1978, 1984 by International Bible Society, used by permission of Zondervan Publishing House, all rights reserved; *The Message: New Testament with Psalms and Proverbs* (MSG) by Eugene H. Peterson, copyright © 1993, 1994, 1995, used by permission of NavPress Publishing Group; the *Revised Standard Version Bible* (RSV), copyright 1946, 1952, 1971, by the Division of Christian Education of the National Council of the Churches of Christ in the USA, used by permission, all rights reserved.

Stanton, Glenn T., 1962-
  My crazy imperfect Christian family : living out your faith with those
who know you best / Glenn T. Stanton.
    p. cm.
Includes bibliographical references.
  ISBN 1-57683-403-4
  1. Family--Religious life. 2. Family--Religious
aspects--Christianity. I. Title.
  BV4526.3.S73 2004
  248.4--dc22

                          2003014981

Printed in the United States of America

1 2 3 4 5 6 7 8 9 10 /08 07 06 05 04

FOR A FREE CATALOG OF
NAVPRESS BOOKS & BIBLE STUDIES,
CALL 1-800-366-7788 (USA)
OR 1-416-499-4615 (CANADA)

Warmly dedicated to
Dr. K. Eric Perrin,
a good man who became a great friend
at a time when I really needed one.

Contents

Acknowledgments

Poetry is written in seclusion, but books typically are written in community. This book is no exception, and therefore I owe gratitude to a small group of friends. Toben Heim, thank you for the idea of a book like this and for asking me to give it a shot. John Paulk served as a critical encourager, sounding board, and idea stimulator when I was creatively stuck at an early stage. J. R. Briggs was another cherished encourager, who plowed a good deal of ground for the book by diligent prayer. I appreciate your friendship. Jim Mhoon, Bill Knott, Jeanie Young, and my wife, Jackie, all read early drafts and offered wise advice. Alison Arant provided very helpful research assistance. Dale Ahlquist, president of the American Chesterton Society, generously helped me track sources for a few quotes. I have yet to stump Mr. Ahlquist with a question on G. K. Chesterton, and I detect he enjoys the challenge. He provides a wonderful introduction to this original thinker at *www.chesterton.org*.

Steve Wade, a treasure of a friend, provided a provocative sidebar for chapter 2 and many memorable and productive hours of conversation over the years on the nature of true spirituality. Life would be richer for everyone if they had a friend like Steve. Hope Radliff, my cherished assistant, graciously helped close loops on a number of practical issues. Brad Lewis, my editor, improved the book greatly.

Much of my learning about the nature of the Christian family comes from many years of observing the wonderful Cobb family in Florida. You are a nearly perfect family because you are so beautifully imperfect. Jackie and I love you dearly and cherish our long friendship.

Jackie, this book would never have been if it weren't for you. My life with you is rich and provides the theater for learning about the nature of family life. Who knew that in all those zillions of hours of debate and conversation, you were helping me write a book. You are a remarkably beautiful woman, wife, and mother in every way. Because of you . . .

WHERE IS THIS BOOK GOING AND HOW WILL WE GET THERE?

Let's start out by understanding something important: The key to loving Christ in your family is not by living out "five easy steps to victorious Christian living" or "seven sure-fire principles to a godly family." It's not "for dummies" and there's no "idiot's guide." Fads and formulas will fail you because Christianity is so much more than tips for a successful life.

Instead, the key to loving Christ in your family is having a colorful understanding of and appreciation for Christ's interest in your family and why it matters in a real flesh-and-blood home. This understanding will serve you well as you seek to serve Christ in the rest of the years that make up your life. It will reveal both the why and the how of being Christian in your family life.

Think of Christ's teachings. People clamored for rules—specifics to live by—so they could know whether or not they were pleasing God. However, Christ taught us that life isn't about following rules or mere behavior. It's about something much bigger: living in the spirit behind the rules. Christ told us it's one thing not to take your neighbor's wife. It's another not to desire her in your heart.

To live Christianly in your family, or anywhere, is getting beyond the rules, and understanding and living in the spirit of Christ. That's what we explore in the chapters of this book.

• Chapter 1 asks what it means to love Christ in our

families, and it launches us into the topics addressed in the following chapters.

- Chapter 2 recognizes that home is often the place where we have the most difficulty reflecting the spirit of Christ.

- Chapter 3 explores why a Christian cares about family at all and how family is a primary part of the Christian story. It also helps us understand how this truth makes our everyday, real-life family routines deeply sacred.

- Chapter 4 begins to address some of the specific issues of family life, starting with sexuality because this is where the family begins. It also helps us answer the question, "How should I, as a Christian, think about sex and how does that understanding make a difference in my life?"

- Chapters 5, 6, and 7 take us into an exploration of what it means to love Christ in the three primary family roles of spouse, parent, and child. Everyone identifies with at least one of these. What does it mean to live out our family lives in these roles? How do we bring glory to God in them?

- Chapter 8 examines some common myths that Christians have held about family life and seeks to get at the truth about the issues behind them. We hold many of these myths because we misunderstand how God works to transform us through family.

- Chapter 9 explores some of the most troubling enemies of establishing and living in a Christian family. This chapter looks at the things that keep us from being what Christ wants us to be in our family.

- As we near the close of the book, we discuss the essential qualities of a Christian home. Chapter 10 shows how qualities like love, Jesus' lordship, and a recognition of the supernatural and the sacredness of the natural serve as fundamental components of our faith. We also look at the roles redemption, holiness, devotion, worship, service, and hospitality play in our lives as followers of Christ.

- In the final chapter, we look at the *key* of living as a Christian in family. This is where the Christian story begins in us, and so we end the book on the most important note. It looks at why we need God, what it is God wants to do in our lives, and how He does it.

This is deliberately not a "cookie-cutter" book. It doesn't pick you up at point A and systematically take you to point Z, where you'll magically be a successful Christian in your family. I wish it could be that neat and easy, but Christian life doesn't work like that. Instead, each chapter offers some essential and major ideas to think about and apply to your life as you seek to live out a love for Christ in your family.

As I think about the approach I take in this book, I'm reminded of that very old adage "Give someone a fish and you feed him for a day. Teach someone to fish and you feed him for a lifetime." My goal is to help you understand the big ideas and how to apply them to your family—to teach you to fish. You can then take these ideas with you and use them for life.

To do anything less is just to give you a fish.

The problem of the family is not a social problem; it is a spiritual problem. . . . [The family] is something so precious that, once broken, it cannot be easily repaired. . . . The solution remains within each family, in the mind and heart of every man and woman. It cannot be otherwise. At the root of every crisis in marriage and family life is the problem of one's own personal life. In a sense, every honest family is a crisis initiated over the earthquakes and hurricanes of human love and romance. . . . Getting into marriage is by definition getting into trouble, and if people keep marrying it is due to the truth that if some happiness is to be found in this life, it is to be found at home.

The family solves the paradox of man, and the paradox that God made man male and female. It also serves the paradox of God, because the warmth of home helps us see that God does not lack that warmth.[1]

ALVARO DE SILVA, BRAVE NEW FAMILY

. . . and so it is.

CHAPTER 1

LOVING CHRIST IN YOUR FAMILY

All right, I will take a chance, I will fall in love with you.

BOB DYLAN, *"IS YOUR LOVE IN VAIN?"*

As a member of humanity, you are unique from everyone else on the planet, but you also have something in common with everyone else. No, it's not that regardless how early you get to bed, you still wake up the next morning feeling a half-hour more sleep would be just right. Or that all the food that tastes best on your tongue lives poorly on your heart, hips, and gut. Or that you can't figure out why anyone likes anything *Star Trek* (or maybe that's just me!).

What you have in common with everyone else is that you are a part of a family. Everyone is someone's son, aunt, sister, father, grandmother, brother, mother-in-law, daughter, husband, uncle, niece, mom, stepfather, or wife . . . something. It's a requirement for membership in humanity.

Some of us have large extended families and some of our families are very small—perhaps only a parent and a child. Some families are remarkably close, and others don't get along well or don't see each other very often—or at all. A few people have no living family members. Whatever your story, we're all part of a family, and these relationships shape us in profound ways.

I grew up in the South in a family with five kids. Once my parents got married in the late fifties, they stayed married. My dad worked for the telephone company his entire working life while my mom ran our home. I had a pretty dependable home life.

Jackie, my wife, was much younger than her three siblings. Her father, Russ, died of a heart attack when she was nine. She tells me he was a very gentle man, and it's hard for me as a father to think of him kissing that precocious little red-haired girl good night for the last time and not seeing her again. Or of that girl remembering the last kiss her daddy ever gave her.

A brother and sister had already married and left the house when Russ died, so Jackie was raised in a single-parent home with another sister. Her mother never remarried and they had a very relaxed, loving home.

Jackie and I met in high school and got married as soon as we graduated. We've been married twenty-one years this year, have put each other through college, and have our hands full with five beautiful, creative, nutty little children. We have our moments (and sometimes days) of struggle and conflict with each other and our children, but our hectic life is usually very happy. Like you, our families have influenced us in many ways—for good and for bad—and we bring those influences into our current family.

Our family is very important to us. And it's a rare individual who isn't concerned about family relationships. We tend to care most deeply for those closest to us; for the majority of us, that's our family. We care about how our family members relate to us and how we relate to them, for what relationships can bring us more immense joy or unspeakable pain than family? If you took a minute to list both your most joyous and your most painful relationships, the people involved would most likely be family members.

This book is for people interested in living well—living Christianly—in their family relationships. It's for people who are curious about two primary questions and how they interplay in the dynamic of family life.

- What is God's purpose in family life?
- How do I live out my love for Christ in my family role?

Answering these questions helps people in the following three groups discover what is central to their idea of family:

- those who already have a living, active faith in and love for Christ
- those who are currently exploring this kind of life, but aren't there yet
- followers of Christ who live in a family with loved ones who don't follow Christ

The goal is to help you understand how serving and loving Christ connects with living out your family role. In the Christian ideal, there's a very tight connection between serving your family in the craziness of daily life and serving Christ. God never intended these to be separate activities.

Briefly, what does this look like? In my family, a large part of living for Christ is realizing that when I made pancakes for my family this morning or as Jackie folds and puts away endless piles of laundry, we're just as surely serving Christ as we're serving our family. For people who have no faith in Christ, these are just activities. But for Christians, they're sacred, and we explore why in these pages. God has many riches for us in these seemingly mundane parts of family life. Frederick Buechner observed, "If God speaks to us at all other than through such official channels as the Bible and the church, then I think that he speaks to us largely through what happens to us."[1] And I believe that, for good and for bad, these things happen most often to us in our family relationships.

God is up to something in your family.

IDEALISM WRESTLING WITH REALISM

To make conversation, strangers I meet while traveling or attending conferences will ask me what I do for a living. When I tell them I write and speak on family issues, I see a look on the face of my questioners and I know what they're thinking. They assume I'm a guy who has family life all figured out. Because that makes me uncomfortable, I come clean right up front.

My interest in family is not rooted in the fact that I have it all together. Quite the opposite. I've been a husband and parent for many years and I'm humbled at the beauty of my family. But for all my experience, the Stanton family is usually careening down the street in the opposite direction of that neighborhood called "having it all together." We've driven through that neighborhood a few times, but we don't own a house there. I don't have any friends who live there either. I'm not sure "having it all together" is a real place with permanent residents. Rather, it seems to be an imaginary land we assume other people live in.

What's an Ordinary Family?

British professor C. S. Lewis kept a longtime correspondence with a woman from America. In one letter, he sought to comfort concerns she had about being an inadequate parent. He told her the only ordinary homes "seem to be the ones we don't know much about, just as the only blue mountains are those ten miles away."[2]

To be honest, I'm often in exile from the having-it-all-together 'hood. I'm amazed (and ashamed) how easily and efficiently I get into trouble with my wife and children on a regular basis. Just the other day, I was downstairs writing in the living room (yes, *this* book on how to love Christ in your family). Jackie was upstairs trying to make sense of the little girls' tornado-strewn bedroom. It was lunchtime and the kids were crying for something to eat.

Because Jackie was making good progress, she called down to ask if I would pull something together for them. I told her I would . . . in just a second. Some disputed amount of time passed (she says it was an hour and fifteen minutes, but it couldn't have been more than forty-five) and still no lunch. Jackie came tromping down the stairs with a certain resonance that got my immediate attention and compelled me to instinctively yell out, "I'm coming right now . . . I've got it!"

What I didn't *do* communicated far more clearly than what I *said*. My lack of action told Jackie her work and progress weren't important to me. It told the kids their needs weren't important. What was important was what *I* was doing. And Jackie wasn't so mad about this particular incident, but rather that this incident was the latest in a consistent succession of such Glenn-centric behavior. Self-centeredness can serve to choke the souls of those around you. And it did in this case.

Some days we live closer to the ideal than others. The trick is to try to have more days in that direction than not. However, the greatest thing we can learn is that those events in family life that exist outside the neighborhood of perfection are some of God's most valuable tools in accomplishing His transforming work in our lives. Think about the most important changes you've made in your life. Conflict with or gentle badgering by a family member probably forced it. Why then would we want to exclude conflict from our lives when we have so much to learn from it?

I write honestly out of the reality of my own family life as I seek to live in and understand the perilous balance between the desire for the ideal and the struggle with the real. With that confession out of the way, let's see how God uses the real to get us closer to His ideal.

WHO IS CHRIST IN YOUR FAMILY?

If we're going to explore how to love Christ in our families, we must ask ourselves the question, "What does it mean to be a Christian?" This helps us be sure we focus on the real deal and not settle for some smaller story. The question of what it means to be a Christian is primarily rooted in who we believe Christ to be and what He desires for us, for Christians have historically been referred to as "Christ-ones," little Christs. And if we are going to be like Christ, we have to have a proper understanding of who He is.

What's in a Name?

Christians weren't always called "Christians." The citizens of the Syrian town of Antioch first gave them this name (see Acts 11:26). It was a term of derision referring to the "Christ-ones" or "Christ-people" who were always talking about loving and serving this man from Galilee. The Christians soon adopted the name as one of honor because this is exactly what they were: "Christ-ones."

To be a Christian in your family means to be a Christ-one, someone who seeks to show forth the character and love of Christ in every part of life.

There are many views of the person of Christ. Some are true to who Christ is. Others are true to who people want Him to be. Sometimes our view is too limited. We seek to put Christ in a box that makes sense to us, a box we can control. And Christ will have none of it.

As Dallas Willard makes clear in his wonderful book *The Divine Conspiracy*, "History has brought us to the point where the Christian message is thought to be *essentially* concerned *only* with how to deal with sin: with wrong doing or wrong-being and its effects."[3] He calls this the "gospel of sin management," and it's much too small a picture of what Christ desires for and from us.

Willard is right. We often fall into the misunderstanding of either the Pharisees or the disciples.

For the Pharisees, pleasing God was all about behavior, about making sure they had the externals nailed down. For many Christians today, it's much the same way. Christianity becomes merely *behavioral* and *directional*. Such Christians have little concern for anything but making sure they're going to heaven when they die (the directional) and managing their sin until they get there (the behavioral).

Regarding the attitude of many of the disciples, Willard explains that they were concerned with something else: the social injustice of the Romans. They saw Christ as their political liberator. He was going to lead them to a just and good society. Other Christians today hold this view. Rather than being concerned only with how people act in their personal lives, they're concerned primarily with social justice—how people act toward others. According to these two spiritual views, Willard says, "A Christian is either one who is ready to die and face the judgment of God or one who has an identifiable commitment to love and justice in society. *That's it.*"[4]

Now let me be *very* clear here. Neither of these is wrong, for Christ is holy, and He wants us to be holy. He also deeply desires for us to share the eternity of heaven with Him, and He loves justice. The Christian life is not less than these things, but it is certainly more. His followers should seek these things. What we get wrong is the *"that's it"* part. Christ is after much more from us than being good, being just, and going to heaven. According to Willard, what Christ seeks in us is "personal transformation toward the abundance and obedience emphasized in the New Testament, with a corresponding redemption of *ordinary life*."[5]

Willard quotes Anglican Bishop Stephen Neill for further clarification: "To be a Christian means to be like Jesus Christ. . . . Being a Christian depends on a certain inner relatedness to the living Christ. Through this relatedness *all* other relationships of a man—to God, to himself, to other people—are transformed."[6] A Christian is someone who seeks to see Christ's majesty lived out in *every* area of life. This includes every aspect of family life.

What does this mean for my everyday family life? It means that the stuff and substance of my Christianity is much more than what I do or don't do, strangely enough. It's more than the movies or shows I don't watch, the words I don't say, the music I don't listen to, the political positions I do or don't have; it's more than the rules I make for myself or my children. Rather, it's about who I love and what I am *becoming* and helping my children *become*. Are we becoming like Christ in every part of our lives, the religious as well as the everyday? Is my family life a growing picture of Christ in the world today?

SPIRITUAL SUCCESS IN FAMILY ISN'T A FORMULA

As we think about what it means to be a Christian and what Christ does in our lives, we must recognize that He meets us as individuals. We can't fashion false christs to our own likings, for the whole substance of the Christian story is that this transaction happens in the opposite direction: We do not make Him into what *we* want *Him* to be; He makes us into what *He* wants *us* to be. Christ draws us to Himself, redeems us, and transforms us as individuals according to His own good pleasure. Our task is to surrender to Him and cooperate as He does this work in us and our family members.

Therefore, we must understand that spiritual growth isn't some prepackaged formula; instead, it's as different as we are and as vast, as creative, and at times as mysterious as God. There is no one-size-fits-all spirituality just as there is no one-size-fits-all family. Regent College Professor Gordon T. Smith explains in his helpful book on spiritual transformation, *On the Way: A Guide to Christian Spirituality*, that as followers of Christ we should all be free from "feeling obligated or burdened by the spiritual pattern of our neighbor. One person's conscience and vision of the spiritual life may lead him or her up one path or across one bridge— and we do not all need to follow."[7] This isn't some postmodern Oprah-anity in which all religious options are equally valid. It's simply the recognition that God does His work in us differently as individuals. Look at the stories of Christ in the four Gospels. Christ interacts with each person as an individual.

Unfortunately, some writers and speakers have whittled down Christian spirituality in family life to very precise formulas: when babies should be fed, how long to let them cry before comforting them, how to do family devotions, how you should school your child (at home, or in public or private school), when and how teens should date, and so on. These teachers map it all so specifically and authoritatively, as if they found a lost tablet of Moses that contained additional commandments.

Forcing how to raise kids or how to build a strong marriage into a narrow formula limits Christ's lordship. Christ doesn't create all children the same. Nor does He crank parents off an assembly line like automobiles with an accompanying owner's manual to tell us exactly how moms and dads are to run. People aren't machines. Marriages aren't cloned. Children aren't blank slates. Each family is a unique creation of God, and He is redeeming each in different ways, all to the same end: to bring glory to the Father through His Son. Don't allow anyone to reduce your relationship with Christ and your family to a list of formulas.

Some Christians buy into these strict programs because, frankly, formulas and to-do lists are easier to follow than trying to figure out what God might have for us as individuals. However, God created us as individuals, Christ died for us as individuals, He redeems us as individuals, and He transforms us as individuals. This book recognizes this fact and hopefully will help you live in what God has for *you* in *your* family.

It's About Glory

In John 17, we have a remarkable opportunity to eavesdrop on God. Jesus shares a moment of intimacy with God the Father just before He is to face the cross, and we get to listen in. Reflect on the first lines of Christ's prayer: "Father, the time has come. Glorify your Son, that your Son may glorify you. . . . I have brought you glory on earth by completing the work you gave me to do. And now, Father, glorify me in your presence with the glory I had with you before the world began" (verses 1,4-5, NIV).

In following Christ, our call is to do what Christ did. He brought glory to the Father on earth by completing the work He was given. We bring glory to the Father by doing the work He gives us to do. This work is, among many things, to serve our family and be Christ there.

No Lone-Ranger Christians

Pointing out the individuality of each family doesn't mean that we can't learn from others about growing more Christlike as a family. That would deny the power and impact of community we find in the body of Christ. Just as there is no one-size-fits-all spirituality, there are no lone-ranger Christians. While Christ created each of us as individuals, He didn't create us to live and grow individually. He grafts us into a community—first our family and then the church—so we benefit from the diversity of that community and draw from its many riches.

We learn this little truth of faith and life from the college student in our Thursday night Bible study and from the saint who works at the drugstore where we get our film developed and from the parents we chat with at tee-ball practice. We learn more from our pastor's preaching as well as from the woman who cleans up after dinners in the fellowship hall and from the guy at the mechanic's garage whom God is slowly but surely healing of alcoholism. And in our families, our own children teach us about the character of God and our parents help us learn what it means to deny self. All together, it's a beautiful mosaic of the story of what God is doing in each of our lives.

That mosaic looks different for all of us and that's part of its beauty. Christ is the common author and artist, yet He distinctively marks each by the unique creativeness, color, and wonder His hand forms. We should have the boldness to learn from others and the confidence to stand in the unique picture God is making of our lives.

HOW DOES GOD USE FAMILY TO ACCOMPLISH THIS TRANSFORMATION?

Family members nag one another. Jackie (lovingly) nags me constantly about watching the kids like a hawk when we go to the park to play or ride bicycles in the street. I nag her (even more lovingly) about watching our budget. We can drive each other crazy. She reminds me to be more patient. I hound her about being more systematic. We both dog the kids about picking up their things.

Family can certainly be a "haven in a heartless world" as one writer put it, but it can also make you want to run screaming into that world. Some believe family is bad because it can be so unpleasant. But British writer and wit G. K. Chesterton finds the *value* of family in this very fact. "Of course," he explains, "the family is a good institution because *it is* uncongenial."

The men and women, who, for good reason and bad, revolt against the family, are, for good reasons and bad, simply revolting against mankind. Aunt Elizabeth is unreasonable, like mankind. Papa is excitable, like mankind. Our youngest brother is mischievous, like mankind. Grandpa is [incoherent], like the world; he is old, like the world. Those who wish, rightly or wrongly, to step out of all this, do definitely wish to step into a narrower world. They are dismayed and terrified by the largeness and variety of family.[8]

Those who consider abandoning family life are dismayed by the fact that family is a demanding discipleship. Our loved ones call us to be something we wouldn't otherwise be. Sometimes they do this gracefully and other times it is quite painful and unpleasant. But God uses both of these processes—the good and the bad—to accomplish the transformation that He desires for each of us. If Jackie didn't nag me toward reform and virtue, I would be a miserable and selfish picture of a man. Christ has used her to transform me, and His work isn't done yet.

Family is life-giving and life-demanding at the same time. This is the ironic nature of family. And within this ironic nature, God works in us. Our families teach us—like few other instructors—that life is not about us. Family forces us to consider the needs and desires of others, and that's part of the change Christ tries to bring about in us. Through family, He says, "Stop seeing yourself as the center of the universe and live for others." This is a fundamental part of reflecting Christ to the world. The German Christian martyr Dietrich Bonhoeffer described Jesus as "a man for others."[9] As Christ-ones, we're to imitate His example. Like nothing else, family helps us to do this.

Christ wants us to be something different than what we are. He wants us to cooperate in the transformation of others. And just as rough stones are polished into gems through friction over long periods of time, family transforms us. It completes us and allows us to participate in the transformation and completion of others.

The trick to loving Christ in your family is to realize the value of your family in Christ's work in you.

What Does It Mean to Serve Christ in My Family?

Serving Christ in your family is all kinds of things you wouldn't think of as service. It is as large as His lordship.

Serving Christ is playing Chinese checkers with your kids, washing the dishes with a happy heart when it's not your job, listening with rapt attention to your mom's story—the same one she told you just last week.

It's working on your sex life with your spouse, teaching your children that Christ was once a child, fighting for your spouse's and children's dignity, changing a flat tire, taking the grandkids to a doctor's appointment, going fly fishing with your brother-in-law, teaching by example how to deal graciously with a busybody neighbor.

Being a Christian in your family means swinging on the tire swing with your daughter, working two jobs to make ends meet, working fewer hours to be with your spouse and children, showing (not just telling) your twelve-year-old daughter how beautiful she is, being concerned about your family's diet.

It's teaching a child how to make shadow puppets, encouraging your wife to finish her master's degree because she wants to, taping your child's artwork to your office wall, admitting you're wrong and apologizing (even to your kids), listening patiently while your spouse complains about a pain-in-the-neck coworker, teaching your children to love books.

It means fixing the vacuum cleaner, setting standards for your kids and sticking to them, telling your son he's got what it takes, letting your child correct you now and then, telling your daughter she's smart, easing off your standards for special occasions, talking to your kids about what makes Van Gogh's paintings so wonderful and encouraging the same spirit in them, coaching soccer.

Serving Christ in your family means changing your father's soiled diaper, making a birthday special, modeling for your children what prayer is, peeling carrots, teaching others to see God's glory in nature, learning to hear from God in the littlest parts of life, kicking out of your house the drug-abusing, stealing child who refuses to change, telling your wife why you are still in love with her, attending open houses at school, learning to love poetry together, having cannonball contests at the pool, cleaning up vomit, holding a crying child, taking your mom to garage sales on Saturday, explaining to your children how Christ entered (and continues to enter) your life and how to be aware of Him seeking to enter theirs.

It means teaching kids to ride bikes, unpacking moving boxes, tending your garden, watching movies together, making pancakes in animal shapes, learning to play the violin, living a flesh-and-bones, honest life in community with other followers of Christ, living a flesh-and-bones, honest life in community with those who seemingly have no interest in Christ, doing carpool, apologizing for being short with your dad the last time he called.

Serving Christ in your family means loving Him in the fullness of the family He has given you in each moment of every day He provides. As Malcolm Muggeridge wrote, "Either all of life is sacred, or none of it is sacred."[10] If some parts of our God-given lives are *not* sacred, then Jesus is *not* truly Lord.

Your family is sacred. Live in it and seize it all!

What Does God Use for His Work?

Eugene Peterson writes, "There is a strong Christian conviction, substantiated by centuries of devout thinking and faithful living, that everything given to us in our bodies and in our world is the raw material for holiness. . . . Nothing in nature—nothing in our muscles and emotions, nothing in our geography and our genes [or homes and families]—is exempt from this activity of grace."[11]

WHY DO WE HURT
THE ONES WE LOVE?

You always hurt the one you love; the one you shouldn't hurt at all.

LARRY MONDELLO ON LEAVE IT TO BEAVER

It's Sunday afternoon and we're trying to decide what to do today. Jackie wants to take some pants for Isabel back to The Gap. It's been bone-chilling cold for the past few weeks and today it's a gloriously unseasonable springlike day, so the kids want to get out to the park and play. Task-oriented, analytical Dad recognizes we have no lunch or dinner groceries for today or the rest of the week, so I make the authoritative declaration that we must get groceries.

Of course, there's nothing wrong with spending part of the day solving a problem. The problem was the way I said it. My tone and body language screamed that any plan not including the important task of getting groceries was stupid. I'm sure my family was asking, "Why does Dad have to be such a jerk sometimes?" I asked the same question.

Why do I do this? I wish I could rewind the tape and try it again. I'd never act like that at work if my team wanted to go one direction on a project and I thought we needed to go another. I'd deal with the disagreement and each person involved with respect and diplomacy.

I've never yelled at a coworker. I've never been snippy to a clerk at the grocery store. I've never insulted a neighbor. I've never made any of the kids at the playground or church nursery cry. So, why have I done each of these—and more—to the people I love most dearly? I'm guessing you ask the same question.

Let's take off the masks and put everything on the table. We all struggle with this problem. Leo Tolstoy opens *Anna Karenina* with a famous sentence: "Happy families are all alike; every unhappy family is unhappy in its own way." It's the same for everyone, just in different ways. Pope John Paul II recognized the earthiness of family life when he said, "There is no family that does not know how selfishness, discord, tension, and conflict violently attack and at times mortally wound its own communion."[1]

And let's put this reality about family life in a larger context. Don't think that God can't relate to what your family is like or that He's *shocked* by the way you behave with one another. Have you checked out some of the families in the Bible? I doubt your level of family dysfunction is anywhere near what we read about there, so don't ever think God can't relate to your story!

Do You Have a Biblical Family?

Wouldn't life be grand if your family was more like those in Scripture instead of like the ones in postmodern America? Actually, no. Have you checked out families in the Bible? It's not a pretty picture. Bible family stories read more like script ideas for *Jerry Springer*.

Really! If a newlywed husband can get booed off TV by a raucous crowd for claiming he didn't impregnate his girlfriend, imagine the jeers Adam and Eve would get for saying it wasn't their fault for bringing sin and death upon the entire population of the world. "Seriously, it wasn't us, it was that other naked garden couple." Nice try. Then there's that little family "issue" of child-on-child homicide.

And the family picture doesn't get any better. In fact, after Adam and Eve, God eventually cleared the board. Noah jump-started humanity again, but things went stale immediately, starting with a sketchy incident in which Noah's son Ham walked in on his drunk, naked, and unconscious father. Noah was humiliated enough to curse Ham and his offspring. (Of course, it seems that being a Hebrew named Ham would have been curse enough.)

Next we find Abram and Sarai trying to "help" fulfill God's promise for a family as numerous as the sands of the sea and stars in the sky. Sarai isn't producing familial fruit, so she develops a plan to have her husband give it a whirl with her handmaiden. They succeed. However, Sarai doesn't take it well, blasts Abram for actually following her advice, and then treats the surrogate mother horribly until she flees.

Then, consider Lot, who apparently didn't gain a "drunk, naked, and unconscious" wariness from his ancestor. He gets sauced and seduced by his two daughters and ends up unwittingly (grand?) fathering two boys from his own girls. Springer would drool for stuff like this!

Lest we forget, biblical families don't only get in trouble while they're naked. Many fully clothed families also provide less than outstanding examples.

Remember, Jacob managed to dupe his brother, Esau, out of his birthright for a lousy bowl of bean soup. In fairness to Esau, it was probably scrumptious. In any case, Jacob came out with the better end of the deal, except that his sons later crushed his spirit when they stripped down their baby brother, Joseph, and cashed him in as a slave to some camel truckers.

Even the great King David, who was truly a man after God's own heart, did time as a liar, conspirator, thief, adulterer, and murderer whose wives (wives?) and children were liars, thieves, adulterers, and murderers. In fact, it's downright challenging to track who slept with whom, who killed whom, and who attempted to kill whom within David's immediate family. They alone could have covered sweeps week on *Jerry Springer.*

In the New Testament, we have sisters Mary and Martha squabbling over the "I'm doing all the work and she's doing nothing!" issue that every parent experiences nearly daily. And don't forget that Jesus came to us from the family line of adulterers and prostitutes.

So, do you have a biblical family? Better hope not.

But don't miss the point: The only perfect family is the Holy Family. There is no perfect human family. Not even in the Bible. Biblical families aren't blueprints for how we ought to be, but they are memos on what we are: fallen people in need of redemption and grace. No human family is beyond sin and its repercussions. No family is beyond needing the grace of Christ, so your family is in good company. And it's never beyond God's love, repair, and use.

Do your best in prayer and action to keep your loved ones off the talk-show circuit. But never forget that family is the prime stage of Christ's redemptive work for you and for your children—and *that* is what being a Christian in your family is all about. (Contributed by Steve Wade.)

So, why do we treat total strangers with more grace and kindness than our own flesh and blood? Why, indeed! Does it mean you have a bad family? Does it mean you or your family members are losers? Or does it mean something else? You might be surprised.

Being a Jerk to Your Spouse

We can act like such jerks to our spouse, the one individual God has given us, above all others, to love and serve. Wives can nag their husbands to no end and husbands can be remarkably insensitive to their brides. Why does this happen? In marriage, God creates a union with our spouse that is so close, so intimate, so inseparable that He declares us one flesh. And we can fight with our spouse as passionately as we can make love, sometimes more so. No one on earth can get us as heated (in good ways and bad) as our spouse, and this is one of the great ironies of marriage. Sometimes our relationship with our spouse is such that, as one man told me, "There are times I feel I would happily trade her for a warm Diet Coke." Yet your spouse is so central to your world that what should be the most wonderful experiences of life are painful if your spouse is not there to share them with you.

A few summers ago, I was teaching a weeklong seminar on family ministry to a class of Koreans training to be missionaries. The class was held at Youth With A Mission's University of the Nations in Kailua-Kona, a splendid little village nestled along a dazzling, blue-green bay on the island of Hawaii.

One evening after a long day of teaching, I strolled down to the village alone, got some dinner, and then ate some fresh-made mango ice cream I bought at a beachside stand. Oh, yes! With my dessert in hand, I sat on a short, weathered stone wall overlooking a remarkable scene. My legs hung over the fence, dangling just above a massive patch of green lawn, which spilled onto a stretch of sugar-white beach melting into a brilliant turquoise ocean.

While I sat there, enjoying the scene, a massive neon-orange sun quietly descended into the water. It all happened in a matter of minutes and it was one of the most glorious things I've ever seen. It was God's magic and it was perfect—but it wasn't. As much as I was gripped by the profound beauty of the moment, I was also gripped by the emptiness of not having Jackie there to share it with me. I didn't think of my children, my parents, my buddies at work. I needed Jackie to be with me, and the moment was actually painful instead of joyous because she wasn't there. Only she means that much to me.

Contrast that with something that happened a few nights ago. It's late in the evening; all the kids have gone to bed except little Isabel, who is toddling around the floor acting like a clown. Jackie is folding clothes on the couch and watching *David Letterman*. I'm at the kitchen table, working on my laptop and concentrating on this very chapter. Jackie interrupts me a number of times to have me watch Isabel as she runs up to the television, smacks David Letterman on the face with both hands, and then runs back to the couch, giggling. To the first three invitations of "Hey, Glenn, watch!" I give Isabel a quick glance and Jackie a brief "ummmp-phhh!" and a nod hoping that will satisfy my paternal duty to be interested in my family right now. I'm in my own zone.

On the fourth invitation, I, with great love and care, yell, "Jackie, can you just quit buggin' me!" It was another one of those moments where I wanted to roll back the tape and get a do-over.

If the most beautiful scene in nature is nothing without my wife, why do I fail to cherish her in the beauty of everyday family life?

Being a Jerk to Your Parents or Children

Our oldest daughter is eight. She's a confident and sweet-natured girl. Lately though, she acts as if she has hit her teen years a bit early. It has us stymied. How can such a big, ugly attitude fit in such a precious little girl? She seems to be telling our household, "I'm the boss here and I'll do whatever I want. If anyone tells me otherwise, I'll wear them down until they see it my way." Do you have kids like that at your house?

Finally exasperated, Jackie and I sat Livvy down and tried to get through to her with a heart-to-heart chat. We tried to help her put her relationship with her parents in context with her relationships with her teachers and friends' parents. Her behavior is flawless with these other adults and she receives compliments for it.

No doubt, she gets part of this from me. I remember my mother scolding me about something when I was a teenager, probably something having to do with a snotty attitude. I can't remember what I said in response, but it was mean, and I remember her slapping my face. It was the first time my mother ever laid a hand on me in anger. As she smacked me, laughter exploded out of my mouth, right in her face. I don't know why I laughed, but there it was. And she cried. I was shocked by my behavior and sad that I hurt my mom.

Why would Livvy speak to us, who she loves deeply, in a way

she would not speak to any other adult? Why would I speak to someone I love so dearly in a manner that would cause her to reflexively strike me—and then laugh in her face? Why would I make someone I love cry? Why do any of us do these things?

Being a Jerk to Siblings

The other evening, after dinner, baths, and the application of fresh jammies, our kids went back to their bedrooms to play together. They played some game contently for the longest time, giving Jackie and me time to sit quietly and talk about the day. After a while, they all emerged from the back of the house and stood before the couch to tell us goodnight. Sophie, our five-year-old twin, had a little name badge stuck to her chest. It was made out of a small, yellow sticky note inscribed with a name written in green marker. It was a part of her role-playing uniform as a checker at a store, a teacher, or something. An older sibling made the nametag for Sophie because she can't read or write yet. As Jackie and I made out what the badge said, we had to fight back the laughter and manufacture a look of parental indignation. It read, "Mrs. Poopy."

The mean things brothers and sisters do to one another.

So, the Question Is . . .

Again, the big question is, Why can we be saints everywhere else, but act like the chief of sinners at home? Let me share some of the reasons I think we act like this and ask you to add your own thoughts to the list.

We're Comfortable at Home

The great British preacher Charles Spurgeon warned, "What we are at home, that we are indeed."[2] Well, among many things, we are sinners. And we're not sinners because we sin; rather, we sin because we're sinners. When Adam and Eve decided to do their own thing in the Garden of Eden and eat the fruit God said was off limits, they infected the whole human race with their selfish "it's pretty much all about me" nature. It runs deep within us. As a result, no family in history has been exempt from the corrupting nature of sin. As humans, it's what we do; it's who we are.

And where are we more ourselves than in our homes? Our families see the fullness of who we are—for good or bad—and they are stuck with us. They can't trade us in for a new family, although plenty have tried to do this in the past few decades as our skyrocketing divorce rates attest. According to the latest numbers, more than a third of all adults aged forty to sixty in the United States have been divorced.[3] But as research has revealed, trying to trade a less-than-perfect family in for a better one isn't the answer. In fact, less than a third of divorces lead to family lives showing *any* measure of improvement, while more than 70 percent lead to families *more troubled* than the one just left—merely trading one set of problems for another.[4]

Do You Have an Unhappy Family?

What's the surest road from a miserable marriage to happiness: divorce, or sticking with it? You may be surprised. Using data from the National Survey of Families and Households, Dr. Linda

Waite from the University of Chicago and other prominent researchers found that two out of three unhappily married couples who avoided divorce or separation ended up with happy marriages five years later. Only one in five unhappy spouses who divorced had happily remarried in the same period. More striking, of those who reported their marriage "very unhappy," nearly eight out of ten who stayed together reported being happily married five years later. Most of these couples didn't seek counseling or marital therapy. They just hung in there and rode out the hard patches of marriage and things got better. As Waite explains, these couples "stubbornly outlasted" the unhappy times, and with time, "many sources of conflict and distress eased."[5]

Like investing in the stock market, hanging in there through the highs and lows of the relationship is more likely to yield big dividends in relational happiness and contentment. Getting out when things look bad is unwise.

Home is where our own kind are. We didn't choose them. They were appointed to us and we're stuck with them. They're the people we're comfortable with. That's why we act like ourselves when we're alone with them.

Remember, one of the chief ends of the Christian life is our slow but certain transformation into the character of Christ. And if God is going to use others to participate in our redemption and transformation (and of course He does), He's going to use those who see where, why, and how we need that redemption. He's going to use those people we live most honestly in front of: our family. I know Jackie and my children are some of the most powerful agents God uses to change me into what He wants for me. I'm guessing that you can say the same of your family.

The Pressures of Domestic Life

I've talked with a number of friends about our tendency toward Jekyl and Hyde behavior. Mike, a buddy from Atlanta who oversees a busy team of magazine editors and is a father of four, says one of the primary reasons he acts this way at home is because of the press of life.

> By the time I get home from work in the evening, I've already given my best for the day. My best energy, my best creativity, my best patience—it has been all but used up by the time I walk through the door of the house. So my family often gets the leftovers and most of the time that's not enough. I'm not as patient. I'm not as enthusiastic. I don't have as much to give. All of that makes it a lot easier to be short-tempered and even ugly with my wife and kids.

Add to this the simple pressure of living in a home with other people. There are bills to pay, toilets to clean, laundry to do, homework to attend to, art lessons to drive to, groceries to buy, meals to prepare and clean up after, teeth to brush (224 in our house alone), stories to read—and the list seems to never end. Who wouldn't lose their cool with such a large and consequential load?

I find that when I am really feeling the pressures of domestic life, that's when I'm most inclined to reveal my "Adamic nature," as the theologians call it.

We Take Grace for Granted

Another reason we can act like grizzlies at home and teddy bears everywhere else is because we fail to appreciate the treasures we have in our families. Our families are familiar (notice the similarity of those two words), and we tend to under-appreciate the familiar. This is the way J. R., another friend (married, no kids yet), experiences it: "My high school coach always said, 'Those we love the most, we treat the worst.'"

Unfortunately, it's true. I believe it's true because we take grace for granted. We carry a basic presupposition that our family will always love us and forgive us, no matter what. While we appreciate this fact, we often abuse it and take our family members—and this truth—for granted.

We must realize that our families are treasures—precious gifts given to us by God. God has called us to care for and love our neighbors; we shouldn't forget that family is our closest neighbor. We share something much more intimate than the same street or community. We share the same flesh, the same heart . . . the same toilet.

Family, immediate and extended, is one of God's greatest gifts. And a gift doesn't have to be perfect. In fact, the imperfectness of the gift is what makes it so valuable. Family is God's greatest tool to transform us into what He wants us to be, and it's where we learn most readily to extend grace. This is the main story of all the families in the Bible. Kevin, a friend, father, and husband from

South Carolina says, "When you see families act horribly to one another and then God still reaches out to accomplish His will through them, you realize that the wonder of His goodness is overwhelming."

A Picture Worth a Thousand Words

Anne Lamott writes in her book *Traveling Mercies,* "There is nothing more touching to me than a family picture where everyone is trying to look his or her best, but you can see what a mess they really are. Frozen in the amber of the photograph, you can see all the connections and disconnections, the stress and the yearning."[6]

Family Relationships Matter

Another reason we can act so poorly at home is because home really matters. No one knows this better than Satan, God's jealous enemy, who wants to mess up God's most important things. Satan probably doesn't care if he can derail a relationship between a plumber and his customer. As much as that relationship matters, it's less central in God's purposes. But family . . . that's another story.

If the Evil One can foil family relationships and get them off track, then he's messed up a major part of God's design. Satan will always vigorously and insidiously attack the things that matter most to God. That is why he attacks us at home and why God's grace is so important there. Remember, God's grace extended to others is Satan's most bitter pill.

WHAT'S THE REMEDY?

So, are we left to be relational boneheads at home, insensitive dolts who treat each other poorly? This behavior will always be part of the picture this side of eternity. Remember what the apostle Paul said in Romans? "I decide to do good, but I don't really do it; I decide not to do bad, but then I do it anyway. My decisions, such as they are, don't result in actions. Something has gone wrong deep within me and gets the better of me every time. It happens so regularly its predictable" (Romans 7:18-21, MSG).

This is the paradox of humanity. But what's the answer? How does Paul find hope in his dilemma? In two ways.

First, immediately following this verse, Paul gives a proclamation of grace and hope: "Therefore, there is now no condemnation for those who are in Christ Jesus, because through Christ Jesus the law of the Spirit of life set me free from the law of sin and death" (Romans 8:1-2, NIV). We don't escape God's condemnation because our families are perfect. We escape His condemnation because we cast ourselves upon and seek to love Christ and His Spirit. And Christ doesn't condemn us when we blow it. He offers us hope in the form of real help.

Second, Paul says, "But those who live in accordance with the Spirit have their minds set on what the Spirit desires . . . [and] the mind controlled by the Spirit is life" (Romans 8:5-6, NIV). We must invite Christ's Spirit to reign strongest where Satan's attack is the greatest. This is at home.

Remember, God doesn't leave us to work this all out for ourselves. We must realize that our hope is found in:

- *The Father who loves us:* First, we have the reality, power, and example of the Father's love. Jesus called Him "Abba," or "Daddy." His heart for us reveals the kind of daddy He is, for He wants us to know that in the midst of our rebellion, "I have loved you with an everlasting love" (Jeremiah 31:3, NIV). And this love isn't based on our behavior, for He continues to love us at our most unlovely. That's *agape* love, the love of God. We're to mirror that love, and we can only do it with supernatural help.

The Four Loves

One of the best treatments of the different kinds of love, particularly God's love, is C. S. Lewis's *The Four Loves* (Harcourt Brace Jovanovich, 1960). An audiotape of Lewis giving a talk on this book (the only commercially available recording of his voice) is worth the price just to hear his beautiful English baritone. It's available at many sites on the Internet.

- *The Son who transforms us:* That supernatural help comes from the transforming power of Christ. We take on this remarkable transforming power by trusting in, communing with, and dwelling in Christ. Gordon Smith writes, "To be a Christian is to be in communion with Christ."[7] Christians follow the chorus of that wonderful Christmas hymn all year round, "O come, let us adore Him, Christ the Lord." Anything else said about being a Christian is a footnote to this point. Christ tells us, "I am the vine, you are the branches; he who abides in Me, and I in him, he bears much fruit; for apart from Me you can do nothing" (John 15:5). And chief among the fruit that Christ wants us to bear is love (see 1 Corinthians 13).

- *The Spirit who keeps us:* The Father shows us that love is possible because it comes from Him. The Son makes it possible because He brings us into relationship with the source of love. And the Holy Spirit, the third person of the Trinity, indwells us and keeps us in that love. It's not our nature to reflect this love, so the Spirit brings "rivers of living water" to flow from the innermost parts of our being (John 7:38).

God, in the fullness of His being—Father, Son, and Holy Spirit—is our hope of living fully in the reality of family life and striving for the ideal. The walk of the Christian life is to

- allow the example of the Father to compel us to a new life of love, kindness, and graciousness;
- allow the transforming power of Christ to change us daily in our home lives; and

- allow the Holy Spirit to keep us from being controlled by our more troubling desires by bringing forth a new spirit of love, joy, peace, patience, kindness, goodness, faithfulness, and self-control within us (see Galatians 5:22-23).

Paul found this answer, and it changed him from a nasty man to a gentle one. What family wouldn't be more pleasant with these wonderful traits growing more abundant? But be sure, these things don't come in a magic, immediate event, but rather in a lifelong growing process.

It's not *easy*, but it is *real*. Our families play a key role in this sacred journey.

WHAT DOES A CHRISTIAN CARE
ABOUT FAMILY ANYWAY?

*So they hurried off and found Mary and Joseph, and the
baby, who was lying in the manger.*

LUKE, THE PHYSICIAN (LUKE 2:16, NIV)

Jackie and I are feeling overwhelmed with family life just now.
It's Christmas, a magnificent time of year for Christians, and
we've had a wonderful time with our children, celebrating our
Lord's birth, exchanging presents, and having a little more relaxed
schedule with breaks from work and school. But even in this
wonderful time, we feel we are drowning in the waves of chores,
duties, and demands that family life relentlessly brings.

Today finds us feeling like Lucy in that classic scene from *I
Love Lucy* where she's working in a candy factory, taking the just-
made candy from the conveyor belt and placing it into boxes. She
hangs in there for a while, but before long the conveyer belt picks
up speed and she starts to fall behind. In spite of her crazy antics
to keep the sweets from dropping on the floor, her frantic efforts
become futile.

Too often we are Lucy. There's just *too much* to do, and we
grow impatient with one another in the midst of it.

But *why* is it this way? I wonder if the primary reason is

because we get caught up in the smaller story of family—the stuff that needs to be done, the chores that need to be accomplished, the care that needs to be given—and we fail to appreciate the larger story that family life is. And most important of all, we fail to see how the family story flows from the Christian story.

So, how should a Christian view family? Conservatives, traditionalists, and liberals all encourage us to take on a particular view of the family for various reasons. Which beckoning should we answer? Where does the Christian's allegiance belong?

By exploring the role family plays in the fullness of the Christian story, we'll discover why a Christian should be interested in family. And remember, it's difficult to love Christ in your crazy imperfect family if you don't have a Christian understanding of why family matters.

WHAT DOES CREATION SAY?

The great Christian thinker Francis Schaeffer said that if the Christian doesn't have a good understanding of what's at work in the first chapters of Genesis, he or she won't be able to understand what's happening and why in the rest of the Bible.[1] Likewise, Pope John Paul II explains, "The family must go back to the beginning of God's creative act if it is to attain self-knowledge and self-realization in accordance with the inner truth not only of what it is but also what it does in history."[2] Both are right. And so, we begin to understand why a Christian should care about family by looking at Creation, because this is where it all starts.

In the glorious Creation story, the Triune God willfully speaks the material world into existence out of nothing. We read that when God saw all that He had made, He declared it was very good. As good as that aspect of creation was, Genesis 1:27-28 indicates that the human family is the crown of all this glory because man and woman together uniquely and beautifully reflect the image of God. No other part of creation reflects God's very image. As such, the family is the first human association and the initiation of culture. We'll look at the larger details of this later, but the primary point is important: The human family is unique in creation and special to God.

ABRAHAM, SARAH, AND THE MAKING OF GOD'S PEOPLE

Consider also the covenant God made with His people, Israel, through Abraham. In Genesis 17:5-7, God said to Abram:

"No longer shall your name be called Abram,
    But your name shall be Abraham;
    For I will make you the father of a multitude of
nations.
    "And I will make you exceedingly fruitful, and I will
make nations of you, and kings shall come forth from
you.
    "And I will establish My covenant between Me and
you and your descendants after you throughout their
generations for an everlasting covenant, to be God to
you and to your descendants after you."

When God promises to make a great nation from Abram, He's not speaking of the way nations are usually founded—through political power or ideological or economic influence. Abraham didn't amass a following by being commanding or persuasive, but simply by being a progenitor. God established Israel, His people, not by converts, but by family.

How We Talk About the Kingdom of God

The words we use when we talk about the kingdom of God also remind us of the importance of family. How do we understand God? The Christian tradition has historically understood that God comes to us as Father. As we've already discussed, Christ the Son refers to God the Father as Abba. *Abba* is an Aramaic word communicating great intimacy and tenderness between father and child, similar to our words *Daddy* or *Papa*. God the Father is gracious and He unconditionally loves and cares for His children. Christ's story of the prodigal son vividly communicates the gentle nature of God as Father. This story isn't so much about the sin of the son, but about the unbounded grace of the father.

The Gracious Father

Henri Nouwen, in his great little book *The Return of the Prodigal Son,* tells of being undone when he saw a poster reproduction of Rembrandt's painting of the same title. It communicated something deep about God to him. Three years later he had the opportunity to go to the Hermitage in Saint Petersburg to study the original painting. He spent more than four hours just sitting and looking at this penetrating work. As the day's changing light shone across the canvas, he noticed what few others do: all the important points and differing physical expressions of the people in the painting—two women, two men, and of course, the welcoming father and the repentant son. Nouwen's book explores what this painting and Christ's parable tell us about God.

Nouwen recounts,

> All my attention was drawn to the hands of the old father pressing his returning boy into his chest. I saw forgiveness, reconciliation, healing; I saw safety, rest, being at home. . . . His outstretched hands are not begging, grasping, demanding, warning, judging or condemning. They are hands that only bless, giving all and expecting nothing. . . . I was so deeply touched by this image of the life-giving embrace of father and son because everything in me yearned to be received in the way the prodigal son was received.[3]

The imagery of family continues as Christians also recognize the second person of the Trinity, Christ, as the Son of the Father.

We enter the kingdom of God by being "born again," as Jesus explained to Nicodemus. This curious phrase caused Jesus' questioner to ask how a man can enter his mother's womb a second time. Christians become children of God, not as direct and natural descendents of Abraham, but through adoption. God adopts us when through faith we accept and trust in Christ's saving death and resurrection for us. Christians will experience the great culmination of the kingdom of God, the *parousia* as theologians call it, at the glorious wedding feast when the bride of Christ, the church, weds Christ the bridegroom.

Consider also that since our faith's founding, Christians have intimately referred to other believers worldwide as brothers and sisters. And Paul explains that the defining mark of a Christian is not holiness, charisma, knowledge, hard work, or sacrifice. Instead, it is love—the primary component of family life and the principal quality of God (see 1 John 4:8). We understand God and His kingdom through the beautiful language of family.

It's not insignificant that God chose to communicate the beauty, truth, and wonder of His holy and glorious project in the language of family. He could have used the languages of politics, commerce, learning, drama, good and evil, etcetera, but He didn't. *He chose family.* And this language wasn't chosen for dramatic effect. God chose it because it corresponds, communicating something really true and beautiful about His nature, His heart, and His relationship with humanity.

What If God Was One of Us?

Singer Joan Osborne had a hit song several years ago in which she asked, "What if God was one of us, . . . just a stranger on the bus, trying to make his way home?" Exactly, Joan! What if God was one of us?

One of the biggest points in considering what Christians should make of family is found in this question. It's answered in one of the biggest events in the Christian story—the Incarnation—God becoming one of us in the baby in the manger who grew to be the carpenter from Nazareth. Yet, while being fully man, He remained fully God. A grand mystery.

The Incarnation, C. S. Lewis said, "was the central event in the history of the Earth—the very thing that the whole story has been about. . . . Every other miracle prepares for this, or exhibits this, or results from this."[4] How did God do this grand miracle, entering our realm as God and as a man? We all know the story, for we celebrate it at least once a year at Christmas.

At the appointed time, Mary, a lowly woman who had great favor with God, and her humble, hard-working carpenter husband, Joseph, were traveling from the nowhere town of Nazareth to the less-than-somewhere town of Bethlehem to participate in the census. While in Bethlehem, Mary, who was "great with child," gave birth to a son in the only place they could find or afford: an out-of-the-way, smelly stable.

God, remaining what He was—fully God—came into the world and became what He was not—fully human—through a common family doing the mundane things families have to do.

Remarkable! Joseph and Mary had to pay their taxes, forcing them to plan and make a long trip to another city when Mary was in no shape to travel. I wonder if they felt a little overwhelmed, like Jackie and I feel today? Could they have related to Lucy at the conveyor belt? They had to find and pay for lodging but could only find a stable because Joseph forgot to anticipate the crowds and make reservations. He had to calm down this spirited, young Jewish mother-to-be in her final hours of pregnancy. Can you imagine Mary's response to Joseph's news? "You want me to have this baby where?!" Picture *your* family on a road trip and then throw in having a baby in a hotel room (or perhaps more accurately, the dog-walking area of a highway rest stop). Imagine the anxiety both Mary and Joseph must have felt. It was in the scenario of this "family moment" that Christ our Savior came into the world. This is a monumental point in our understanding of family. Don't ever think that God can't relate to your family life when it gets a little too "real."

Of all the grand and glorious options at God's disposal, He chose to do an incredibly miraculous thing in a seemingly ordinary way. He entered our realm through a family—an ordinary family that no one took notice of. This is an incredible stamp of approval upon the whole family enterprise: the relationships, the work, the struggles, the warmth, the logistics, the emotions, the love, and the immense comfort.

Of the Incarnation

In the Collects of *The Book Common of Prayer* (1789), we read, "O God, who didst wonderfully create, and yet more wonderfully restore, the dignity of human nature: Grant that we may share the divine life of him who humbled himself to share our humanity, thy Son Jesus Christ; who liveth and reigneth with thee, in the unity of the Holy Spirit, one God, for ever and ever, Amen."

Please don't pass over this point too quickly! Pause for a while and soak up the implications of this glorious reality. God chose to present His only Son to the generations of the world upon the stage of a common family doing common things. And consider this most important question: What does this fact say about God's view of family life and what does that mean for your participation in family relationships? This is so important that you should seek to answer this question for the rest of your days, for it is deep, profound, and full of riches.

JESUS WAS A FAMILY MAN

God came into our realm as an infant in a family, but this wasn't just a convenient or dramatic entrance. Jesus, the God-man, remained active in family life for the length of His days on earth. We seldom reflect upon the first thirty years of Jesus' life, before He started His public ministry, because Scripture says so little about those first three decades. Does this mean we should be unconcerned with those years because they have nothing to offer? I think the very fact that Scripture *doesn't* record much of His early life is significant because it reveals there wasn't much that seemed worth recording. For the first thirty years of Christ's life, He simply lived a normal, mundane human life—learning and working at a trade, caring for His mother, making and enjoying friends, growing and living in a community.

Scripture says He studied at synagogue, showing wisdom and understanding far beyond His years. But tradition tells us He would have learned the carpentry trade from His father and most likely helped Joseph run the family business. We assume He played games with other children. It doesn't take much imagination to picture Him doing chores around the house and woodshop. Surely, He took pleasure in completing a nice table and delivering it to a customer's home. He felt frustrated when the customer was late in paying, when His tools broke, or when a supplier tried to gouge Him for materials. He swept up endless piles of sawdust. He sweated and got splinters in His fingers. He fetched water for His mother and went with her to market. He helped friends move into new homes. He fished. He came to the aid of neighbors whom others took advantage of. He spent time alone with His Father. He got tired and enjoyed meals with friends and probably didn't care for having to clean up afterward, but often did so with a gracious heart. God did all these things.

Of course, we don't know specifically what He did, because Scripture doesn't tell us. But for the first thirty years of His life, God, in Christ, was content to do the daily family-life things everyone does.

I often wonder why it took Christ so long to start His ministry? If this was the really important part of His life—teaching and saving humanity—why did He take so long to get to it? Remember, in those days, there was no adolescence as we know it. Tradition tells us Mary was in her early teens when she was pregnant with Jesus. So, at thirty, Jesus was nearly two decades into adulthood. Why did He wait to get on with His work? It seems as if Christ was content just to linger in everyday life, day after day, for thirty years. That says something very profound to the Christian about normal family life.

Again, please don't move over this fact quickly. Stop and ponder this truth for a good while. The consequences are profound! In Christ, God was content to linger in family life. His identification with and participation in it sanctifies the whole endeavor, making it holy and spiritual—for whatever God does is holy and spiritual. Think about that tonight as you peel potatoes or carrots, do dishes, sweep floors, or fix the hinge on a broken door. God did those things too and didn't see them as a waste of time.

Jesus was a family man. Family relationships and duties were a part of His life until His last day. Among His final words from the cross was a request to His friend John to care for Mary after His death. God's participation in all the cares and duties of family life means that Christianity does something no other religion or philosophy does: bridge the divide between this world and the other world, bringing together the physical and the spiritual into a unity. This is why the idea and reality of the Incarnation is so powerful.

All of these—the special place of family in creation, God founding His people through father Abraham, the significance of family in the language of the kingdom of God, as well as in the Incarnation and the daily life of the Savior—reveal that family *does* matter in the Christian story. But it doesn't tell us *why* family matters. That's what we'll look at now.

THE NATURE OF GOD AND HUMANITY

Genesis 1:26-27 is one of the most important parts of Scripture. In these two verses we learn some foundational truths about the nature of God as well as humanity: "Then God said, 'Let Us make man in Our image, according to Our likeness. . . . ' And God created man in His own image, in the image of God He created him; male and female He created them."

What does God say about Himself here? Notice the plural

pronouns *Us* and *Our*. God is a plurality, one God manifest or revealed in three eternal, co-equal persons: Father, Son, and Holy Spirit. This community of persons—the Godhead—desires to create something in their own image and likeness. So the Three make humanity, expressed in male and female.

Another important verse of Scripture illuminates what's happening here, yet we seldom reflect on what it really means. Genesis 2:18 says, "The LORD God said, 'It is not good for the man to be alone'" (NIV).

God says this of Adam, before sin entered the world. But how could anything be "not good" for Adam when he was so fresh from the creative mouth of God? He had unhindered access to God and a beautiful world to live in. What else could he need?

God wasn't admitting a mistake in His design. He was revealing something important to us about the nature of God and man, something we just learned from Genesis 1:26-27. It wasn't good for Adam to be alone because in his aloneness he didn't mirror the image of God who, as Trinity, is relational in His very essence. Because God is not solitary but Trinity, He is a community of intimacy, passion, and love. Therefore, intimacy and love is the core of the universe.

We further understand the sacredness of male and female when we consider that Father, Son, and Holy Spirit are all fully God, co-equal, and eternal. Yet each has qualities distinct from the others. The Father isn't the Son and the Son isn't the Holy Spirit. As God, they have the same essence but different manifestations. And none of them can be understood in isolation from the others. Their differences complement each other.

Likewise, what is Adam without Eve, this other co-equal being that shares the same essence of humanity but in a different physical, psychological, and emotional way? Adam without Eve doesn't fully reflect the nature of God. And that, as God says, is not good. Eve completes Adam and Adam completes Eve. Male and female—different in person, but the same in human essence—are the first two members of a human trinity. Though separate beings, they're one flesh in marriage. They are a mystery and just what the other needs.

The Mystery of God and Man

Think about Adam in his aloneness. As man, he was made with certain distinct qualities. But without Eve, certain things just didn't make sense, if you get where I'm driving. Adam, in his aloneness, is a physical and emotional oddity. He can't be fully understood and can't express the fullness of his God-given humanity without Eve. In a different way, Father, Son, and Holy Spirit can't be understood apart from each other. Each is fully God, but the mystery is that none can be understood in isolation from the others.

Likewise, men and women, as individuals, fully bear the image of God. You do, your neighbor does, your mother and father and the cab driver who speaks an unintelligible language do—each individually bears the image of God. But in another mysterious sense, in our aloneness we don't mirror the Trinity. We're completed by a spouse, an Adam or an Eve, and in this union we most fully bear the image of God—or more properly, the Trinity—for it is not good for man to be alone.

But what about singles? Can they not fully bear the image of the Trinity? They most certainly do as the fruit of the male and female union, being the third member of this human trinity of mother, father, and child. Singles also bear this image as they marry a spouse or are married to Christ and live out their gift of celibacy. Christ becomes their completion.

What's the third part of this human trinity? The answer is found in Genesis 1:28, where God blesses Adam and Eve and bids them to be fruitful and multiply. Male and female come together as one flesh in the sexual embrace and out of that fabulous union comes fruit bearing and sharing their same flesh: children. Mother, father, and child are a glorious human trinity—a glorious mystery.

To illustrate this mystery, I think about what my family is doing right now. I'm at my desk, writing this very sentence. Jackie is downstairs in our family room putting away Christmas decorations. Our kids are all in their rooms asleep in their beds (at least that's the plan). Though we're all in different locations, doing different things, we're all one flesh.

In spite of imperfection, my family, just like yours, is the closest of anything on earth in likeness to the glorious, eternal, and holy reality we know as the Trinity. While every part of creation demonstrates God's glory, nothing reflects the *image* of God like a family.

We weren't made for solitude! We're made for love and intimacy with the Triune God and with other humans. That's why, short of death, solitary confinement is the worst punishment we can impose upon human beings. It's why loneliness and rejection are so unspeakably painful. The opposite is also true. A century of medical, social, and psychological research shows that adults and children are more likely to thrive in every measure of well-being when they're in permanent family relationships.

The Health of Relationship

We are made for relationship. Therefore, we shouldn't be surprised that a huge body of scientific research spanning more than a hundred years consistently shows that married people and their children are more likely than people in any other relational category to enjoy substantially higher levels of physical and mental health, recover from illness quicker and more successfully, live safer lives, report higher levels of overall happiness, earn more money, have better sex, and experience significantly lower levels of domestic and general violence. In fact, pick any indicator of adult well-being, and it will show that married adults are likely to have higher scores than other people.

Likewise, children living with their biological or adoptive married parents are more likely to do better in *every* measure of academic success, to stay in school and out of trouble with the law, to resist premarital sexual involvement, and to have elevated levels of physical and mental health. Science finds that people thrive when they're living in committed, lifelong relationships like marriage.[5]

At the end of his play *No Exit,* John Paul Sartre says of hell: "There's no need for red-hot pokers. *Hell is — other people.*" While we may sometimes identify with that, he got it exactly backward. Hell is not other people. It may be more like *not having* other people; aloneness is the opposite of the very nature of the Triune God in whose image we are made. We're not made to be alone.

How the Christian Story Can Help You in Your Family

Why does understanding the biblical basis for family matter? Because to love Christ in our families, we should understand what we're participating in and why it's important. Understanding these realities can revolutionize our understanding of and participation in family by bringing the glory of God and heaven down to the commonness of family life and by lifting the commonness of family life up to the glory of God.

God's incarnation in Christ and His participation in family life sanctifies the whole family process. Whether we realize it or not, we're all participating in and proclaiming the glory and mystery of the Trinity in the world by simply being someone's child, wife, or husband. As such, we're mysteriously bound to others as one flesh. With this understanding, it makes sense to ask why we'd break these relationships through abortion, divorce, desertion, abuse, or infidelity. We must understand that when we do tear these relationships, we break far more than appears on the surface. We break others, ourselves, and the Trinitarian image in humanity.

As Christians, we should be able to recognize the profound significance in family, cherish it, and allow it to illuminate our lives. And this isn't true only when we're doing what we typically think of as spiritual or religious. We proclaim this beautiful reality simply by virtue of our participation in it.

When Jackie and I recognize and remember this reality, it helps us get through days when we feel overwhelmed with the press of family life. We need to recognize that it's not all for nothing. Because we're participating in what our Lord participated in, He can identify with our struggles. And because this is true, we also need to recognize and appreciate that the mundanity of the family routine isn't something we should try to escape or merely tolerate, but rather something very sacred and worthy of celebration.

This puts washing dishes, paying bills, cleaning clothes, helping with homework, fixing broken toys and appliances, brushing teeth, and all of what it takes to run a household in a whole new light.

Family is very big stuff. Live in it!

CHAPTER 4

SEX: WHERE IT ALL STARTS

*Sexual lovemaking between humans is not and cannot be
the thoughtless, instinctual coupling of animals; it is not
"recreation"; it is not "safe." . . . Because it is so powerful, it is risky . . . because it requires a giving away of the
self that if not honored and reciprocated, inevitably
reduces dignity and self-respect. The invitation to give
oneself away is not, except for the extremely ignorant or
the extremely foolish, an easy one to accept.*[1]

WENDELL BERRY

A few years ago, we were living in the deepest part of the deep South. Late on a Tuesday afternoon in the middle of January, I was working at my downtown office when nice, big, north-of-the-Mason-Dixon-line kind of snowflakes started to fall softly. Cool!

I watched the snow come down outside my window for about twenty minutes when April, my assistant, popped her head in my office and recommended we all think about trying to get home before it got too bad. *Too bad?* I thought. *It's impossible for snow to get too bad at this latitude.* But it was a good excuse to get off work early and maybe have enough daylight to romp in the snow with the kids. So we all headed home at 3:30 as it continued to get worse. What was usually a twenty-minute commute took me three and a half hours that day. The snow just kept coming! Those light and innocent flakes became a winter scene you might see from Buffalo, New York, on the Weather Channel. It kept up until late into the night.

The next morning, all the streets were impassable. Safety officials gave the whole town a mandatory snow vacation; without snowplows, we had to wait for the sun to clear the roads. So the Stanton family used our three (three!) snow days to watch movies, read books, take naps, and just not worry about the rest of the world. Jackie and I passed some of that time enjoying each other.

Four months later we found ourselves in Jackie's OB-GYN's office looking at our fifth child on an ultrasound machine. A nice little product from those lost days of work productivity.

The ultrasound technician commented that they'd been very, very busy lately, busier than ever, and she wasn't quite sure why. I asked her if she remembered how long it had been since we'd had that big snowstorm. I saw her blush as an "ah . . . so that's it!" look washed across her face.

Our world has been forever altered because Isabel Stanton came into the world, splendid fruit of the lovely union shared between a husband and wife on a pristine winter afternoon. And because of all the other babies conceived over those days . . . and every day.

Sex, for good and bad, can be "awe-fully" consequential. As such, it is always provocative and never safe. When Andy Warhol said, "Sex is the biggest nothing of all time," he was so wrong. Sex is one of the biggest *somethings* of all time—and for far deeper reasons and in many more fabulous ways than most people appreciate.

For Christians, sex is a big thing because it's a big thing to God.

Those outside the circle of faith often see followers of Christ as we typically see our parents. They couldn't possibly be sexual, save for the few obligatory engagements needed to bring offspring into the world. But this is a false understanding. Truth be told, parents and Christians have a very vibrant interest in sexuality (except my parents, I'm sure!). And Christians have a higher view of human sexuality than most people. G. K. Chesterton hinted at this in an odd way when he said, "When once you have got hold of a vulgar joke, you may be certain that you have got hold of a subtle and spiritual idea."[2]

And Bruce Marshall is even more startling: "The young man who rings the bell at the brothel is unconsciously looking for God."[3]

What Chesterton, always the provocateur for truth, is trying to have us understand is that human sexuality comes to us from God, and even when it is sadly perverted in a vulgar joke, the teller is unwittingly referring to something that is, at its root, remarkably sacred and godly. (And that's exactly why the perversion of it is so wrong.) Marshall would have us know that even the search for intimacy in the wrong places, in the wrong ways, is ultimately about seeking what God made us for. (And that's exactly why it should be sought in the right places in the right ways.) This search drives all of us in many different and powerful ways. Some are simply more aware of what is really behind it.

What these men are saying is that—at its root as God created it—sex is remarkably sacred and ultimately about seeking that which God made us for. We must understand that God's interest in human sexuality is so much more than merely making sure people *behave* themselves. God is much more than some supreme Dr. Laura barking out moral directives over a heavenly radio. Sure, His take on sex includes right behavior, but it's not confined to only this. His interest is rooted in something much bigger.

God, and those who follow Him, take sex very seriously, and the Christian picture of sexuality is much more serious, vibrant, and well . . . sexy . . . than any other view held in the larger culture. As a result, it's far more fulfilling.

While it might seem old-fashioned or passé to people outside the faith, the Christian view of sexuality is actually a very radical one. It's radical because it goes against the culture and holds up human sexuality as nothing less than an icon of the inner life of God. That's far from "nothing." Before we address this, let's understand the place of sexuality in family life.

THE GATE LEADING TO THE HOUSE

Regarding the relationship between sex and the family, allow me the indulgence of quoting Chesterton again:

> Sex is an instinct that produces an institution; and it is positive and not negative, noble and not base, creative and not destructive, because it produces this institution. That institution is the family; a small state or commonwealth which has hundreds of aspects, when it is once started, that are not sexual at all. It includes worship,

justice, festivity, decoration, instruction, comradeship, repose. Sex is the gate of that house; and romantic and imaginative people naturally like looking through a gateway. But the house is very much larger than the gate. There are indeed a certain number of people who like to hang about the gate and never get any further.[4]

Sex certainly isn't an end in itself, any more than a gate is an end. It leads us somewhere. Sex ushers us into something grand and glorious, more than we can imagine. Therefore, we need to understand its nature and participate in it as it was meant to be. C. S. Lewis refers to this when he says, "The monstrosity of sexual intercourse outside of marriage is that those who indulge in it are trying to isolate one kind of union (the sexual) from all the other kinds of union which were intended to go along with it and make up the total union."[5] A Christian view of human sexuality is all about context — making sure we don't separate some parts of the thing from all the others that are intended to make it a complete thing. *The Message,* Eugene Peterson's paraphrase of the Bible, states it this way:

There is more to sex than mere skin to skin. Sex is as much spiritual mystery as physical fact. As written in Scripture, "THE TWO SHALL BECOME ONE." . . . We must not pursue the kind of sex that avoids commitment and intimacy, leaving us more lonely than ever — the kind of sex that can never "become one." There is a sense in which sexual sins are different from all others. In sexual

sin we violate the sacredness of our own bodies, these
bodies that where made for God-given and God-modeled
love, for "becoming one" with another. (1 Corinthians
6:16-18)

Again, we accomplish this not by merely understanding how we
should act or not act, but how human sexuality reflects the very
inner life of God and how it gives Him glory when we live in it as
He created it.

WHAT IS GOD'S INTEREST IN SEX?

As we saw in the previous chapter, Adam as man and Eve as
woman are uniquely created to show forth the image of God in
creation. They reflect it as individuals and they reflect it as com-
plements to one another. This image is one of love, intimacy, creativity, cooperation, beauty, glory, and much more. In Adam and
Eve's God-given design, let's observe how their sexuality is a primary part of their being.

What's the first statement God makes to Adam and Eve after
their creation? "God blessed them; and God said to them, 'Be
fruitful and multiply, and fill the earth'" (Genesis 1:28).

Think of this in terms of what He *doesn't* tell them to do.
From the start, God doesn't tell Adam and Eve to engage in

- learning, as intellectual beings,
- prayer, as spiritual beings,
- economics, as industrious and productive beings,

- politics, as orderly and civil beings, or
- writing stories, performing music or dance, or doing art, as creative beings.

Of course, each of these is part of our God-given humanity and part of God's command to "subdue" the earth. Each of these is a part of family life that we should practice and celebrate. But these are not what came first. God blesses man and woman and bids them to be fruitful and multiply—*exercising and reveling in their nature as sexual beings.* This was the first command for humanity, and Adam and Eve were, no doubt, quite happy to obey. God was pleased also.

Likewise, let's look at the event when Adam and Eve, fresh from the mouth of God, first gaze upon each other. Adam didn't look at Eve and declare his appreciation for her intellectual brilliance, her sensible outlook on life, or her spiritual piety. Not by a long shot!

Adam and Eve first glory in something else, something some Christian theologies have unfortunately and incorrectly thought of as quite base and ungodly. They marvel at each other's bodies—their flesh. When Adam sees Eve for the first time, he proclaims with great excitement, "This is now bone of my bones and flesh of my flesh" (Genesis 2:23, NIV).

He can't help but recognize this aspect of her. God had made Eve beautiful and Adam knew instinctively that this partner was just right for him. Adam was a physical and emotional oddity without Eve, but now it all made sense. Both of them understood the naked truth (sorry!) that Adam was made for Eve and

Eve was made for Adam. God revealed it in their flesh, as part of His perfect design.

What Role Does the Physical Body Play in Discipleship?

George MacDonald wrote, "It is by the body that we come into contact with Nature, with our fellowmen, with all their revelations to us. It is through the body that we receive all the lessons of passion, of suffering, of love, of beauty, of science. It is through the body that we are both trained outward from ourselves, and driven inward into our deepest selves to find God. There is glory and might in this vital evanescence, this slow glacierlike flow of clothing and revealing matter, this ever uptossed rainbow of tangible humanity. *It is no less of God's making than the spirit that is clothed therein.*"[6]

In *Mere Christianity*, C. S. Lewis said, "There is no good trying to be more spiritual than God. God never meant man to be a purely spiritual creature. That is why He uses material things like bread and wine to put the new life into us. We may think this rather crude and unspiritual. God does not: He invented eating. He likes matter. He invented it."[7]

This helps us understand something very important about Christianity. As C. S. Lewis said, "Christianity is almost the only one of the great religions which thoroughly approves of the body—which believes that matter is good, [where] God Himself once took on a human body."[8]

This makes it difficult to sustain the gnostic view of humanity held by many Christians, who believe "the flesh" is a lower or baser part of our humanity and our soul or spirit is a higher and godlier part. How can this be, when from the beginning our physical bodies are very much a part of God's perfect picture of humanity—before Satan's corrupting hand came on the scene? This gets us back to Chesterton's quip about the vulgar joke. Satan can corrupt sexuality and the flesh and turn it into something ugly. But it is, at its core, something beautiful and godly. Therefore, the flesh *is* spiritual and we should appreciate and cherish it under the lordship of Christ.

Human Sexuality As a Picture of the Inner Life of God

When God said, "Let us make man in our image, in our likeness (NIV)," and then created Adam and Eve and bid them to be sexually fruitful, it tells us something important about who God is. I don't want to draw too sharp a comparison here, because the persons of the Trinity don't have physical bodies as we do and therefore don't manifest their love for one another as humans do. But notice the close connection in the tight space of two short verses (Genesis 1:27-28) of God's desire that we reflect the image and likeness of the Trinity and how God directs Adam and Eve first to commune with each other as sexual creatures.

We can't overlook the significance of this: God creates man and woman as reflections of the image of the Trinity and the first command is to engage in the sexual embrace. This means that when a man and woman come together in marital sexual intimacy, somehow—mystically—they mirror the wonder, beauty, and creative power of God like no other part of creation. Again, this is far from "nothing." As poet-farmer Wendell Berry explains, "The sexuality of community life . . . is centered on marriage, which joins two living souls as closely as, in this world, they can be joined." He continues, "This joining of two who know, love, and trust one another brings them in the same breath in the freedom of sexual consent and into the fullest earthly realization of the image of God. From their joining, other living souls come into being, and with them great responsibilities that are unending, fearful, and joyful."[9] Beautiful! This is the glory of family life.

Linger on how great this reality is. When Jackie and I find a quiet moment from our little ones, and we're not too exhausted (Jackie often wonders if that is possible for me), and we come together in that time of special communion, it's remarkable to think of what image we're reflecting. It can be overwhelming. No other faith has such a powerful and dynamic view of sexuality.

HOW DO WE LOVE GOD IN OUR SEX LIVES?

For Christians, single or married, this is one of the most important questions we can ask, because our sexuality is so central to who we are. It always made me laugh inside when I was a teenager and church leaders would talk to us about sexual health and encourage us not to be sexually active until we were married. Of course, this was smart and godly advice. But I found it funny because, even though I had never been intimate with a girl and didn't plan to be until I married, I was a healthy teenage boy. I was so hugely active sexually—on the inside, even if there was no external expression. Things were churning in me like a volcano.

I had to govern my feelings and desires constantly. I had to keep my mind from wandering where it shouldn't. I had to be careful how I related with girls and of the images I saw in magazines and on television. Mentally, I was very sexually active. And my sexual, physical, and spiritual health demanded this deliberate, internal discipline to ensure that my outward behavior was in line with what God desired for me. What I'm saying is that we have to see "sexual activity" as so much more than just "doing it." It involves how we appreciate and live out our own God-entrusted sexuality. We are all sexual beings.

I can see this in my preschool-age children. They've already come to a place where they're instinctively shy about family members seeing them naked. When they go from their baths to their bedrooms, they're sure to wear a towel or dash as fast as they can and try to cover themselves by putting one hand in back and one hand in front of them in a futile attempt to keep anyone from seeing their bums. They've become aware, all by themselves, that certain parts of their bodies should be kept private. This is healthy, age-appropriate sexual activity.

So, not only married people should be concerned about loving God in their sex lives. We all have an awareness of our sexuality and how we express it. It's part of our thought life, the way we dress, the ways we interact with boys and girls in our youth and men and women when we're older. It's even a part of how we view and interact with God.

How *do* we love God in our sex lives? We love God in our sex lives by making sure they reflect the nature and qualities of the relationship shared by the Trinity, the image we and our sex lives were created to reflect. This requires that we understand some primary characteristics and qualities of the Trinity.

- The Trinity is a community of lovers who are *relationally active,* not static. They are, from all eternity, giving to and receiving from one another in unconditional, loving intimacy. It's their very nature to do so. It's who They are!
- This community of loving persons is *permanent,* for They have always exhibited this giving and receiving of love for each other and always will. These are not merely convenient or passing relationships.
- This community of loving persons is *committed,* for Their relationships are not dependent on how fulfilled They are or on what They can get out of the relationships.
- This community of loving persons is *exclusive,* for there have always been three specific members and there always will be three. No more, no less. They don't invite other gods into their intimacy nor do They swap partners. They are each for the others.
- The persons of this community are *self-giving,* for They seek to serve and to give to one another and glory in doing so. They're not self-seeking. While They glory in receiving love from one another, it's not about what They can get but what They can give.
- This community of persons is *one,* but also *distinct and complementary.* This means that while the

members of the Godhead are one in essence (each is fully God), They are also distinct from one another and complement one another. Each person of the Trinity can't be fully appreciated apart from the other two. Each needs the others because They are distinct from the others. They complement each other in their uniqueness.

HOW WE DISHONOR GOD IN OUR SEX LIVES

We can dishonor God in our sex lives just as we can dishonor Him in any other area of our lives. We dishonor Him when we serve ourselves. We dishonor God in our sex lives when we fail to mirror the Trinitarian reality and beauty in our relationships.

God's instructions for our sexual lives serve Him by bringing Him glory when we obey them, and they also benefit us. God's rules are not limiting prohibitions, but rather ennobling, enriching guidelines. As theologian George Weigel explains, when we view God's directives for our sexuality this way, "the first moral question shifts from 'What am I forbidden to do?' to 'How do I live a life of sexual love that conforms to my dignity as a human person?'"[10]

This explains why Christian prohibitions against certain sexual practices aren't based on reactive moralism in an effort to keep us from having fun. Quite the opposite! They're based on how we can flourish in our God-given humanity and how we best reflect the image of God in us.

As reflections of the nature and qualities of the Trinity, our sex lives should be shaped by the qualities of the Trinity. Three primary principles apply to all of us and, if we keep these in mind, they'll guide us in a life that is pleasing to God and beneficial to our families and ourselves.

1. We May Never Use Another Person As an Object, Sexual or Otherwise

The members of the Trinity never relate to each other as objects, to be used for their own good. They relate to each other in love, seeking to serve the goodness and glory of the other. Love is a self-donation. It never uses others as things or an end.

When we use others, we diminish their dignity as well as our own. Animals do this. People shouldn't, because it's not what we were created for. It's not what sex was created for. This is why pornography, masturbation, and rape fall outside of God's intentions for us.

Pornography dehumanizes sexuality and depersonalizes people by turning the viewer into a taker and the one viewed into an object. The danger is that we start to see others in our lives the same way we see the object in the magazine, movie, or website: as a nobody, a thing that exists for our pleasure. It also dehumanizes the user because we are made for intimacy with the other sex and intimacy can't occur with illusionary images. It should take place with another person—a spouse.

Similarly, sex is much more than mere physical stimulation. God created it to be a very intimate communion between two people. Therefore *masturbation*, like pornography, is incomplete because it doesn't involve the communion of two self-giving people, one to another. It's sex for one and isn't God's ideal for us; it's merely taking from one's self and doesn't mirror the nature of the Trinity. No member of the Trinity turns in on Himself in any manner.[11] Their relational expression is always to the others. Remember, God said it was not good for man (or woman) to be alone, and in sexualized form, that's what masturbation is.

The Magic Number

As Bob Dylan astutely observed in a recent recording (as only Bob Dylan can), "You can't make love all by yourself."[12] Love requires a community of at least two, and proper sexual love requires no more than a community of two.

Rape isn't about sex, but about control and domination. It's about taking by violence. It's always wrong because it's the complete opposite of what love is. It's one of the most egregious violations of the Trinitarian ideal and, therefore, of human dignity.

2. The Monstrosity of Premarital and Extramarital Sex

The human sexual embrace, this most intimate and ultimate of all human giving and vulnerability, ought to take place in a union of total and permanent surrender of two people. That's what marriage is: both the public and personal dedication of a man and woman to forsake all others and give themselves fully—body, mind, and spirit—to another.

Therefore, to give someone

- our *body* without exclusively giving him or her
- our *mind* or *will* (total, unconditional, willful commitment) or
- our *spirit* (emotions, affections, and adoration)

is to isolate one kind of union, the physical, "from all the other types of unions which were intended to go along with it and make up the total union," C. S. Lewis said.[13] That's why sex outside marriage is a monstrosity. Extramarital sex dissects us at our deepest level, giving out one part of us without giving all the rest intended to go with it. It's not what we're made for.

Where did we ever get the idea that we can separate our bodies from our minds and spirits and that our bodies could do whatever they like without consequence for the rest of our being? This is why the sexual revolution has been such a dehumanizing failure, diminishing our God-given humanity in painful ways. Theologian Karl Barth expressed this well when he declared, "Coitus without coexistence is demonic."[14] We can't connect ourselves with someone sexually without connecting all the rest of our being. Wendell Berry laments, "Because of our determination to separate sex from the practice of love in marriage and in family . . . our public sexual morality is confused, sentimental, bitter, complexly destructive, and hypocritical."[15]

Only the sexual embrace *within marriage* mirrors the nature of the Trinitarian relationship in creation. In the ideal, it's loving, permanent, exclusive, and self-giving. Premarital and extramarital sex can't mirror this reality. This is why it's not surprising research shows that faithfully married people enjoy the deepest levels of sexual satisfaction.

The Best Place to Have Sex

The leading scientific research shows that sex is most satisfying, both physically and emotionally, when confined to the protective harbor of marriage. Scientists consistently find that married couples are most likely to rate their sex lives as "very satisfying" both physically and emotionally, compared to people in any other type of relationship. And who among the married reported the highest levels of sexual pleasure? Couples who have only one lifetime sexual partner and have a vibrant spiritual life together experience the highest levels of sexual fun and satisfaction. In fact, levels of sexual satisfaction declined as the number of lifetime sexual partners grew.[16] Sex is one of the only things in life that doesn't get better with diverse experience. Premarital virginity and wedding rings and active relationship with God are the most powerful sexual pleasure enhancers.

Who would have known? God did!

---

3. The Challenge of Homosexuality

Male and female are not cultural constructs but God-created parts of humanity made for each other to show forth the image of God in the world. Remember Genesis 1:27: "God created man in His own image, in the image of God He created him; male and female He created them."

Male and female, together, are the fullest picture of the image of God in creation. That's why they need each other. Adam wasn't complete without Eve. In everyday terms, this means that only the difference and the complementary interplay of male and female uniquely reflect the image and likeness of the persons of the Trinity in creation. As a result, sexual love between a married man and woman is a life-giving act of mutual giving and receiving that mirrors the Trinity like nothing else on earth. Homosexuality denies this and falsely states that differences in male and female don't really matter. Nothing could be further from the truth. Homosexuality violates the Trinitarian image of complementarity in a profound way.

All sexual sin is wrong because it fails to mirror the Trinitarian image, but homosexuality does more than fail. It's a particularly evil lie of Satan because he knows that it overthrows the very image of the Trinitarian God in creation, revealed in the union of male and female. This is why this issue has become such a flashpoint. It will become even more contentious because nothing else challenges this image of the Triune God so profoundly and thoroughly as homosexuality. It's not what we were made for.

Can Sexual Sin Be Forgiven?

Even as homosexuality, as all sexual sin, challenges the image of God in creation and the purposes for which He created man and woman, this doesn't diminish in any way God's ability and desire to forgive sexual sin. God's desire for your redemption is far greater than the sting of your sin. I have many dear friends whom God has rescued from the practice of homosexuality and has lovingly brought to a place of sexual wholeness. He desires to do it and He can.

Likewise, I have other friends whom God has healed of horrible struggles with heterosexual addictions and issues of infidelity. These healings haven't been easy or quick. But they have been real.

Remember Christ's story of the lost or prodigal son and the loving father (see Luke 15:11-32)? God is the loving father and we are the lost prodigals. When the son came back home, the father didn't ask about all the horrible things his boy had done and then decide whether he could forgive him or not. It didn't matter. What mattered was that his son wanted to come home and the father welcomed him with glad tears. The father's response even shocked the good brother who stayed around. God's grace is boundless, and He desires to welcome any heart that seeks Him—no matter what sin lies in your past.

We love God in our sex lives by living in the fullness of what He intends for us. This has both positive and negative aspects. Positively, we're to live fully as the sexual beings God has created us to be. He wants that for us because we mystically show forth a primary part of the nature of God. But He doesn't give us an unqualified green light. There are stoplights and caution lights we need to pay attention to as described previously. These are not given because God is a killjoy, but for just the opposite: He wants our relationships to mirror His image and likeness. He knows this is best for us, for it's how we're created and what will bring us joy.

Teaching Our Children to Honor Christ
in Their Sexuality

Who's responsible for teaching the next generation how to understand the nature of sexuality, to possess the bigness of it, and to make good decisions leading to healthy and fulfilling sex lives? Schools, the church, MTV, Dr. Laura, or Planned Parenthood? Some of these would certainly be better than others, but the real answer is easy. Parents are the proper ones for this job, and research shows they are most effective.

A major study published a number of years ago in the *Journal of the American Medical Association* examined key factors that contributed to healthy adolescent sexual decision-making. The study found that high levels of parental connectedness (expressed in warmth, love, and caring from the parents) as well as parental disapproval of their child being sexually active or using contraceptives were significantly associated with those adolescents postponing sexual activity.[17]

Another study, a review of five years of research, found that parents who set moderate, reasonable rules for their teens saw the lowest levels of sexual activity among their teens. The study reported that parents who set moderate rules "carefully supervised their teenagers in regard to whom they dated and where they went, and insisted on a reasonable curfew." Interestingly, those parents who offered "very strict parental discipline and too many rules about dating" experienced higher rates of sexual activity among their teens than parents who set larger, more general guidelines—but less than those who set no rules. Also notable was that this study found that parents were "rated high-est in terms of influence on sexual opinions, beliefs, and attitudes, but lower than friends, schools, and books as sources of sexual information."[18]

What do we need to remember when teaching our kids about sex?

- The "sex talk" isn't a one-time event you have with your children at a certain age. It's a lifelong learning process that takes place continuously at age-appropriate times. Tess, my three-year-old daughter, was learning about this when she asked Jackie a very funny question. Jackie was nursing our littlest child (a process we call "numma-numma") and Tess was watching Jackie inquisitively. After their nursing days, most of our children have been raised on rice milk because of dairy allergies. Intently watching Jackie nurse Isabel, Tess asked, "Mamma, do yer numma-nummas have wice milk or wegula milk?" Children naturally won-der about our female and male bodies and how they work. We should guide that wonder in healthy and godly ways.
- When your kids are young, don't answer more ques-tions than they are asking. When they ask why mommy is different from daddy, answer them in a clear but simple way. However, as they grow, and rela-tive to their development and maturity, it is important for parents to dive deeper into some of these subjects.

Between nine and twelve, children should get a pretty
good idea of what sex is about and why it's special.
This brings us to the next point.

- Be sure to help your children understand that sex is
about more than behavior and plumbing. Help them
see God's bigger picture. Our sexuality encompasses
the totality of our being: body, mind, and spirit. It's a
special gift from God that helps us share love, make
new babies, and reflect His image in the world.

- Be sure your child develops a positive view of sex. I've
heard from Christians who have sexual problems in
marriage because they couldn't understand how something could be *bad* before the wedding and *good* after.
These people had a merely moral view of sex rather
than God's view of sex. Help your children see that sex
is always good when it's kept in God's plan. Help them
understand that God gives prohibitions against certain
kinds of sexual expression for our good, to enhance
our God-given humanness. God is interested in what
is good for us, not in keeping us from having fun.

- Remember that your children are learning about sex
when they interact with you and see you interact with
your spouse. Confident girls who aren't easily manip-
ulated by opportunistic boys usually have fathers who
warmly affirmed them and taught by example that
men treat women with respect. They don't have to go
looking for male affirmation in all the wrong places.
Mothers (and fathers on their behalf) who demand

respect from their sons raise those boys to respect and care for women. Your child's future spouse will thank you for raising such a confident, well-adjusted mate for him or her.

• Help your children understand why it's important to guard and protect their sexual purity: it's a key part of their physical, emotional, and spiritual integrity as well as a precious gift they'll one day give to their husband or wife.

• Remember to set reasonable rules and expectations for your children and help them develop an internalized value system that they possess for themselves. It's much stronger for your teenager to be able to say, "I choose not to have sex before I'm married because my sexuality is too valuable to give away to someone who just wants to score" than "I can't because my parents (or church) say its wrong."

Help in Shaping Your Child's Sexual Character

One of the most important but least understood jobs of parenting is making sure you raise a sexually healthy person. In my opinion, the best books on shaping the sexual character of children and helping them establish a biblical view of sexuality are by Stanton and Brenna Jones:

• *How & When to Tell Your Kids About Sex: A Lifelong Approach to Shaping Your Child's Sexual Character.*

This book helps parents understand that sexual education is lifelong for children and that it should encompass not just "plumbing," but all the spiritual, physical, and emotional aspects of sexuality.

- *The Story of Me*. Designed for children ages three to five, this book lays an age-appropriate spiritual and anatomical foundation for understanding God's intention for sexuality.
- *What's the Big Deal? Why God Cares About Sex*. Written for children ages eight to eleven, this book helps children find answers to basic facts about sex and why God created it.
- *Facing the Facts: The Truth About Sex and You*. Designed for kids ages eleven to fourteen, this book equips kids to understand that God intends sex for marriage, discusses love and dating, and answers questions that young people will be facing as they mature in the teenage years.

(All are published by NavPress and you can order them by calling 1-800-366-7788 or by visiting www.navpress.com.)

A GLORIOUS STORY

Christians have a far more beautiful story to tell about the glorious nature of human sexuality than any other story occupying the cultural stage now or ever. None of the rivals are even close. The Christian story of sexuality is true to the fullness in which God made us as humans and true to the nature of what is ultimately behind everything in the universe: God, who is love and who dwells in loving intimacy. We shouldn't be shy about telling it with the power and beauty of our lives.

- We tell it to the world when we make deliberate decisions to protect our sexual health and wholeness from the ravaging wolves of premarital and extramarital sex.
- We tell it to our spouses when we give our total selves exclusively to them, desiring to give and serve rather than to take. We tell it when we affirm, honor, and protect their femininity or masculinity, whether we're alone or in front of others.
- We tell it to our spouses *and* children when we honor our spouses with our fidelity. This isn't just physical, but also mental and emotional. Husband, do your wife and children see you looking at other women or treating other women more kindly than you do your own wife? Wife, do you use sex as a bargaining chip with your husband, even playfully: "If you don't play golf this Saturday, maybe we can see what happens after the kids go to bed"? Married couples should give of themselves freely and exclusively, without demanding from one another.
- We tell the Christian story when we treat our spouses as reflections of God upon the earth, not as objects for our own pleasure or usefulness.
- As your friends and children observe your life, what do they learn about sexuality? Do they get a distinctly

Christian picture of sexuality? Do they see that you seek to please God and reflect His nature by honoring and serving your spouse? How we quietly care for and live out our sexual lives in front of others is a powerful lesson to them about how we view God, others, and ourselves. Remember, there's much more to our sexual lives than the activity that takes place behind closed doors.

I started this chapter talking about snow and how it brought us the gift of our last child. As I think about that surprise, pristine blanket of snow that covered our neighborhood that week, I think of purity. Loving Christ in your sex life means being pure. It means being chaste. Purity is so much more than what you *don't* do. *It's who you are.* Both purity and chastity are positive virtues and not merely an absence of wrong behavior. Pope John Paul II describes chastity very nicely in one of his pastoral letters:

The chaste person is not self-centered, not involved in selfish relationships with other people. Chastity makes the personality harmonious. It matures it and fills it with inner peace. This purity of mind and body helps develop true self-respect and at the same time makes one capable of respecting others, because it makes one see in them persons to reverence, insofar as they are created in the image of God and through grace are children of God, re-created by Christ who "called you out of darkness into His marvelous light" (1 Peter 2:9).[19]

To love God in our sex lives means to be pure in the fullness of the person God created us to be—physically, emotionally, intellectually, and spiritually. To do so is to live in wholeness.

I am a parent. I am a spouse. I am someone's child. I am a sibling. One thing that all of us have in common is that each of us identifies with at least one or more of these categories.

Think about the enormity of your family relationships, the substance of their being, and the implications of their existence. I'm amazed by what relationships have brought to my life and what they've connected me with.

When Jackie and I first held hands so comfortably and effortlessly on a crisp November evening in 1979, did we have a clue what chain of events we were initiating? When we first spoke our love for one another, did we appreciate what we were proclaiming? As our relationship grew, did we know what we were building?

When I proposed our marriage almost three years later on a balmy summer evening in Florida, did I have any idea what I was getting into?

When we slipped simple gold bands on each other's fingers before God, our parents, and our friends, did we have any understanding of what we were promising and establishing at that moment?

Did we have any idea what was going on in heaven and earth when we became husband and wife?

Did we notice how the balance of the universe shifted when two became one?

When we came together later in that glorious entanglement of flesh and spirit, did we comprehend the mystery at work within us and in the world?

Could we appreciate what we were founding? When time found us wondering aloud if the years would treat us well, did we have any idea how they would change us in far different, deeper ways than we could ever imagine?

When we, through the years and trials of infertility, finally saw that little line on the pregnancy test turn from a red negative to a positive plus-sign (and then four other times in five years), did we have any idea how we were affecting eternity?

As Jackie and I love each other and our magnificent children in a zillion different ways and teach them to love this Three-Personed God, to love other people, and to participate in the redemption of God's creation, do we have any concept for the enormity and the eternal ramifications of what we are participating in?

As we fight with each other for our relationship and the way we think life ought to be, do we grasp the damage our hurtful words do because they're spoken from a lover? Do we realize we're fighting for something that matters beyond imagination and therefore something that is relentlessly under assault by an evil one who despises it with passion?

I don't think we do. I'm not sure anyone ever does . . . or could. In relationships, what we're each involved in is unspeakably deep, mysteriously sacred, and breathtakingly beautiful . . . even if it doesn't always seem that way from appearances.

Outside of the inner life of God, these relationships are the most consequential things going on in the universe.

I am unshakably convinced of it.

CHAPTER 5

BEING SOMEONE'S SPOUSE

*The wedding rings did not stay in the window. The
Jeweler looked into our eyes. Testing for the last time
the fineness of precious metal, he spoke seriously, deep
thoughts, which remained strangely in my memory.
"The weight of these golden rings", he said, "is not the
weight of the metal, but the proper weight of man, each
of you separately and both together. . . . "*

 *Andrew takes one of the rings, I take the other, we
take each other by the hand—my God, how simple
this is.*[1]

         KAROL WOJTYLA, THE JEWELER'S SHOP

Jackie and I were very young when we got engaged. We fell in
love in high school, dated for a few years, and got engaged as
soon as we graduated. We couldn't wait to marry.

 On the evening I proposed, I picked up Jackie from her job
at a children's clothing store at the mall. I took her to our favorite
restaurant and afterward, while sitting in my beat-up '69 VW
Bug, I reached under the seat, pulled out a small box holding a
very humble diamond ring (the diamond was what they sweep
up off the floor after cutting regular-sized diamonds), and asked
her to spend the rest of her days with me as my wife. Without
hesitation, she said, "Yes!" What a glorious partnership we established at that moment.

We were so excited and wanted to tell someone, so we went over to the home of our friend Bruce. While we were telling him the news, his parents came home. They were nice people who loved us greatly. The mother was especially gracious toward Jackie.

When Bruce told his mom our grand news, she was standing just in front of Jackie, who was sitting in a wing-back chair. The mother held out her arms and said, "Oh Jackie, dear, I'm so happy for both of you!" and then she proceeded to fall right onto Jackie like a great redwood felled by a woodsman. Her legs never buckled.

Mrs. Hoffsteder drank heavily sometimes, and she obviously had that night at dinner. When she drank, she got overly senti-mental, weepy, and hyper-motherly. It drove her sons crazy, but they pretended it didn't bother them by making jokes.

As she lay upon Jackie, she looked like she could have slept there for the night. I still remember the look on my new fiancée's face as she peered around the body of this kind woman. Jackie gently patted her on the back, at a loss for what to do. Trying hard to mask his embarrassment, Bruce yelled at his mother, "Mom, for cryin' out loud, get off Jackie!" Later that week, Bruce yelled to us in a crowd of friends, "Hey Jackie, come over Friday night and I'll have my mom fall on you again." We all knew it was both funny and sad.

The coming together of these two events—our new engage-ment and Mrs. Hoffsteder's sad insobriety—is an apt intersection for thinking about the nature of marriage. The formation of a marriage is serious business because it creates a definite trajec-tory, jettisoning you into a world of immeasurable joy or one of great pain—and sometimes both. How could Jackie and I make sure we built our marriage toward joy?

The answer to that question is found primarily in the answer to another question: What is God's job for me as a spouse? This is a question every married person should ask, as well as anyone considering marriage. Sadly, I think we've lost two important things in our culture today. The first is the answer to this question and the second is the desire to even ask it.

Wedding bands are precious gifts husbands and wives exchange on their wedding day and wear until . . . These bands show symbolically what it means to be married. A deep thinking and creative Polish bishop named Karol Wojtyla (pronounced *voy-tee-wa,* later to become Pope John Paul II) explored the power of the wedding band in a play he wrote many years ago titled *The Jeweler's Shop.* It's the story of three couples, each with relationships of differing health and quality, and of their interaction with a jeweler who serves as an instructor in the durability of the sacrament of marriage. Another teacher in the drama is Adam, a mysterious character who comes in and out of scenes to help the couples understand the larger dynamic of their relationships. Toward the end of the play, Adam tells the couples, "Sometimes human existence seems too short for love. At other times it is, however, the other way around: human love seems too short in relation to existence—or rather, too trivial. At any rate, every person has at his disposal an existence and a Love. The problem is: How to build a sensible structure from it?"

Marriage is that sensible structure that brings existence and love together. The character of Adam continues: "But this structure must never be inward-looking. It must be open in such a way that on the one hand it embraces other people, while on the other, it always reflects the absolute Existence and Love, it must always, in some way, reflect them. That too, is the ultimate sense of your lives."[2]

So, what does it mean to be married? For one thing, it means that you are giving yourself exclusively to another in every way, without reserve. The wedding band is a durable symbol of that promise. Maybe you remember this description from premarital counseling or vows. The shape of the ring—an unbroken circle—demonstrates the unending love and faithfulness that makes up the substance of the relationship.

The strength of the precious metal signifies the durability of the love, constant through good times and bad, through feelings of passion, indifference, and even seasons of intense dislike. The purity of the gold or silver represents the selflessness of the love of the couple that "does not seek its own" (1 Corinthians 13:5) and the integrity of the physical and emotional faithfulness to forsake all others and give themselves exclusively to one another in every way. This commitment isn't based on emotion or feeling, for these are fleeting and will fail us. As Erich Fromm explains in *The Art of Loving,*

> To love somebody is not just a strong feeling—it is a
> decision, it is a judgment, it is a promise. If love were
> only a feeling, there would be no basis for the promise
> to love each other forever. . . . Love should be essentially
> an act of will, of decision to commit my life completely

to that of one other person. This is indeed, the rationale behind the idea of the insolubility of marriage.[3]

Wendell Berry agrees: "The difficulty is that marriage [and] family life . . . do not depend exclusively or even primarily on justice—though, of course, they must all strive for it. They depend also on trust, patience, respect, mutual help, forgiveness—in other words, the *practice* of love, as opposed to the mere *feeling* of love."[4]

Why Wedding Bands?

In ancient times, some cultures used rings of precious metal as currency—as symbols of promise to enter and fulfill a contract. During the second and third centuries, Christians started exchanging wedding bands inscribed with symbols of their faith. The unending circle signified the unending commitment of marital promise. The gold or silver represented the purity and strength of the relationship.

This practice continued until the Middle Ages, when another custom was added. The priest would declare to the couple and their community, "I unite you in wedlock in the name of the Father, the Son, and the Holy Spirit. Amen." As he spoke this, either he or the bridegroom would place the ring on the thumb of the bride with the words "in the name of the Father," on the index finger with the words "and of the Son," on the middle finger with the words "and the Holy Ghost," and finally on the ring finger with the "Amen."

I Give Thee My Troth

As Christians, we're not our own. We belong to another, One we cannot see. As spouses, we are not our own. We belong to another, one we can see. And in the Christian ideal of marriage, we both belong to Christ, no longer as two, but as one. This is marked by giving our troth.

What is *troth*? It's an odd word from Old English that communicates the biblical ideal of a husband and wife who forsake all others (physically and affectionately) and live for one another. It means "loyal or pledged faithfulness: fidelity." As James Olthuis explains in *I Pledge You My Troth,* "Troth is the staying power which gives special joy and color to intimacy in family, friendship, and marriage. Troth is the moral expression of love just as justice is its jural expression and thrift is its economic expression."[5] In other words, troth means that when we're married, we can't have other emotional or physical relationships with the opposite sex. We're not free agents. We're not on the market. We have no interest in expanding our options.

We're slightly more familiar with another word that comes from *troth: betroth.* To be *betrothed* is to promise to make this larger promise—to give your troth—to another at some later date in the marriage ceremony. To be betrothed is "to affiance" (from which we get our word *fiancé*) or to promise faithfulness to another.

While we understand that in marriage we're not to give ourselves to others emotionally or physically, we're less inclined to realize that this means we should place our spouse before our family and even ourselves. When we selfishly think about how our marriage or spouse is or is not serving *us*, we're actually not being faithful. We're not giving our troth. Instead, we're only being faithful to ourselves.

The Quality of Christian Love

Carefully read 1 Corinthians 13 (especially verses 4-8) and notice the quality of love Paul describes there. Think of the place you, the lover, hold in this kind of love and think of the place your beloved holds. Love is always about the other person. And this isn't some emotional sentimentality; it's deliberate and intentional.

In addition, if we seek the happiness and approval of our parents over our spouse, we're withholding our troth. We're failing to "leave our parents" and cleave to our spouse as God commands in Genesis. We're failing to live in God's ideal.

In many significant ways, being someone's spouse is to cease to be your own person. But in this giving of yourself, you don't cease to be. Instead, you mysteriously become more than you were. As Andrew, one of the characters in *The Jeweler's Shop*, reflects on his own betrothal to Teresa, he observes, "Love [and marriage] can be a collision in which two selves realize profoundly they ought to belong to each other, even though they have no convenient moods and sensations. It is one of those processes in the universe which bring a synthesis, unite what was divided, broaden and enrich what was limited and narrow."[6]

Becoming More than We Were

A profound mystery of marriage is that by denying ourselves and giving ourselves to another, we become much more than we were. It's not only that "two are better than one because they have a good return for their labor," as Ecclesiastes 4:9 tells us, but also that in losing our lives, we gain them. We're created for others; therefore, it's not surprising that we thrive when we're given to others. If more people understood this, we would have more genuine joy in the world.

Your Marriage: A Picture of Christ and His Church

God's Word tells us that marriage is a mystery (see Ephesians 5:32). Marriage is an earthly, human echo of the glorious heavenly union between Christ the bridegroom and His bride, the church. We don't fully understand how this works. As Paul tells us, the mystery is great (in the sense that it is both wonderful *and* large). But as marriage shadows that heavenly ideal, we know it should be:

- *Holy*—for Christ is pure in all He does.
- *Sacrificially loving*—for Christ laid down His life, which was demonstrated when He girded Himself and washed the feet of His followers, and ultimately when He went to the cross. At every moment, He was driven by His love for His Father and His bride.
- *Passionate*—Christ isn't static or stoic toward His bride, but intensely passionate.
- *Faithful*—Christ doesn't entertain additional relationships. He's trothed to His church. Nor does He tolerate

His bride having other lovers. He is a righteously jealous lover.

- *Permanent*—Christ doesn't remain dedicated to His bride for "as long as it works." If that were the case, He'd have divorced her long ago for her unfaithfulness. But He remains dedicated to bringing her to Himself.

Your Marriage: A Picture of the Trinity

As we discussed in the previous chapter, marriage is also a picture of the inner life of God as seen in the Trinity. In the same breath that the Triune God declared His desire to make man in His image, He created them male and female, blessed their union, and called them to be fruitful by participating with Him in the creation of a new human generation and by subduing the earth. This union (male and female) with the mandate (to create and raise new life as well as to care for creation and establish the fullness of human culture) is the likeness of God's image as He intended. Male and female—coming together in marriage, establishing family, and being active in culture—uniquely show forth the image of the Trinity on earth. We don't understand precisely *how* this is, because it's a mystery. But we know *that* it is, and this truth should revolutionize our understanding of and participation in the nature and work of marriage.

Your Marriage: A Picture of the Cross

Your marriage is also a picture of the cross and Christ's service there. I don't mean that marriage is like a crucifixion, although many social commentators have tried to make us believe that. But it does require us to exhibit the attitude of Christ, who sacrificed Himself, literally, for His bride. We read in Philippians 2:5-8:

> Have this attitude in yourselves which was also in Christ Jesus, who, although He existed in the form of God, did not regard equality with God a thing to be grasped, but emptied Himself, taking the form of a bond-servant, and being made in the likeness of men. And being found in appearance as a man, He humbled Himself by becoming obedient to the point of death, even death on a cross.

We're the image of Christ in our marriage when we empty ourselves in humility and give ourselves fully to our spouse. As a husband, I struggle with this so much. Whenever I have broken my wife's heart and caused her some emotional pain, the root of it is usually that I'm more interested in serving my own needs and wants than in sacrificing for her. It's impossible to cause that kind of pain in someone when you follow the example of Christ. I find it necessary to ask for His help daily to have this attitude within me.

Marriage is the only relationship in human civilization where one person publicly commits himself or herself to live for the good of another, without regard for his or her own well-being. Marriage is a living, earthly picture of the sacrificial nature of the cross of Christ.

Remembering What We Promised

We love Christ in our marriages by honoring our vows. On our wedding day, we face our beloved, take his or her hand,

and before God and the world we declare:

> In the Name of God, I take you to be my wife/husband,
> to have and to hold from this day forward, for better for
> worse, for richer for poorer, in sickness and in health, to
> love and to cherish, until we are parted by death. This
> is my solemn vow.

The giver places a ring on the ring finger of the other's hand and says:

> I give you this ring as a symbol of my vow, and with all
> that I am, and all that I have, I honor you, in the Name
> of the Father, and of the Son, and of the Holy Spirit.[7]

How are you doing in keeping that original promise to your spouse?

THE DAILY GRIND AND THE SPIRITUAL VIBRANCY OF YOUR MARRIAGE

We've been talking about some pretty lofty ideals of marriage. In fact, Christianity has the highest and most vibrant ideals concerning marriage of any religion or belief system. But we don't usually live in these lofty places. Instead, we live in the nitty-gritty daily grind of life. We live in the struggle to fulfill our God-given family and cultural mandates: holding down a job; gaining an education; coaching tee-ball; being a soccer mom or dad; doing laundry;

cleaning, feeding, disciplining, and playing with children; caring for neighbors—all to take care of our little part of God's garden. The tasks are unending.

How do we keep our spiritual and relational vibrancy in the midst of this grind? The thing to remember is that we shouldn't make a distinction between the "worldliness" of the daily grind and the "spirituality" of rising above it. Remember, busyness in work was a part of God's creation before the Fall. God gave us work to do. In fact, busyness and work were part of the scene *before* the creation of humanity. God was busy working for five days, creating the physical world, and then He created humanity and the animals of the land on the sixth day. Contrast the busyness of His labor during the six days of creation with the rest God took on the seventh day. All of this—activity and rest, engagement and retreat—is a part of God's worldly week. Work isn't a curse. Because of the Fall, work seems futile and unnecessarily difficult (see Genesis 3:17-19). But work and busyness are, in their essence, godly and sacred things. We show forth the nature of God when we follow His example of balancing work and rest. God places us and calls us to participate in this cycle that He's created, so it's all "good."

The Goodness of Labor

Even while the Preacher in Ecclesiastes tells us that work is futility and vanity, he proclaims: "There is nothing better for a man than to eat and drink and tell himself that his labor is good. This also I have seen, that it is from the hand of God. For who can eat and who can have enjoyment without Him?" or, as the New

International Version states it, "A man can do nothing better than to eat and drink and find satisfaction in his work. This too, I see, is from the hand of God, for without him, who can eat or find enjoyment?" (2:24-25)

Work is futile if we fail to see it as from God. But when we work hard in family life and then rest to enjoy the fruit of our labors, we're imitating God and living in His design for us.

As Christ did on earth, we're to engage in the normalcy of life. Like Christ, we're also to retreat and spend special, intimate time with the Father. But the Fall, being real and pervasive, makes it very difficult to keep work from becoming tyrannical and choking out the quiet rest of intimacy—with God or our spouse.

To find balance, we should recognize the sacred blessing of laboring with a spouse and having a helper to share in the pain and joy of daily life. As they find and build a new home and family, husband and wife are participating in something far more profound than appears at the surface. (And remember that newlyweds don't start a family when they have kids. They *are* a family; children are additions to that established family.) They're not only building a physical structure in their house or a human institution in their family, but also a home in the coming together of the two. As G. K. Chesterton said, "The human house is a paradox, for it is larger inside than out."[8]

Jackie and I have difficulty remembering this, with all the clothes that need washing and the fingernails and toenails that need clipping—oh, not to mention the meals to prepare, stories to read, homework to be done, grass begging to be cut, training wheels to remove from bikes, and on and on. It can be overwhelming. But every once in a while, we get a glimmer of the phenomenal mystery and sacredness of all this activity. We're living in the midst of something that is both human and godly, and unspeakably profound. We must see that it is from God and be thankful for and proclaim His nature that's revealed in it. *Doing so is true spirituality.*

We must simultaneously protect our marriage against the corrosive effect of the busyness of work and home, and also glory in the holiness of it. This is found in the proper balance of work and rest. It's found in the balance between seeing work as a means of merely earning money or keeping our house in order and seeing it as our God-given task of subduing our part of His garden.

THE SOIL OF YOUR SPOUSE'S HEART

Jackie and I can have a Jekyl and Hyde marriage. We love each other deeply, and there's no other person we would rather spend time with. But honesty is good here. There are days when we wonder how we ended up together. Sometimes we quarrel nearly every weekend. And, wow, can we fight passionately. But there are also seasons when everything is more than marvelous.

We've talked about how helpful it would be to go to a counselor to work through some of our relational garbage. But there seems to be too little time and too little money for such things. Then those storms pass and we realize our troubles weren't rooted in any deep, dark issues, but simply in the fact that life gets stressful and we need to learn to deal with each other more graciously in the midst of it all. We realize that the health of our marriage really comes down to the question of how we're caring for each other's hearts.

The condition of the human heart isn't static. It's constantly in process. In this light, I think of my wife's heart as a garden and I am a gardener. She plays the same role in my life. Am I cultivating the soil of her heart to be dark, rich, and life-giving, or hard, dry, and barren? I have a great deal to do with its condition. How are you tending the soil of your spouse's heart?

We create beautiful garden-hearts in our beloveds when we love them without condition, when we seek their well-being above ours, when we support them when they are down or hurting, and when we rejoice with them on top of life. We create healthy hearts in them when we listen to them with our hearts and our ears, when we have more faith in their abilities and talents than they do, and when we encourage them to chase their outermost limits.

We cultivate hearts of hard bitterness when . . . well, when we fail to do the stuff just mentioned. We build contempt in our spouse when we expect and take without regard. We build bitterness when we treat others as objects. We create hearts of hardness when we do what I did the other night.

As I was packing for a business trip, Jackie and I were talking about how we could help a friend of mine who was in some legal trouble. Jackie, who was lying on the bed, was very interested in helping me resolve the problem and asked me about all the various angles, implications, and possible resolutions. One of her gifts is helping me analyze the deepest of issues. Problem was, I needed to get up early the next morning to catch a 6:30 flight, and I wanted to bring the whole discussion to a close—but I didn't say so. When she asked another probing question, I answered her as if I'd already told her five times in five minutes that I didn't want to talk about it anymore. Before I even realized what I said, how I said it, and how hurtful it was, I saw the look on her face. It said, "Why would you treat me like an enemy when I'm trying to help you?" It was a good question. She rolled over and turned her back on me.

One incident like this won't harden my wife's heart, but a regular serving of it will. And I'm afraid I do it far too often. I have to be ever mindful of this because of what it does to my dear wife's heart. It's my duty to tend the garden of her heart in a life-giving way.

Being a Spouse Means . . .

Loving Christ in your family means loving Christ in your spouse. As a spouse, you're involved in something much bigger than merely a relationship with another person, for marriage is far greater than the sum of the two individuals. To be a spouse is to be transcendent. Being a spouse means:

- You belong to another. You're not your own. You commit yourself exclusively and completely to another person. And you express your love in giving your body, your energies, your affections, your emotions, your attention, your fidelity, your protection, your honesty, your self. And in giving to this exceptional other, you become more than you are.

- You give your troth, your willful commitment to give all of yourself through everything life throws at you or takes away. You don't base this commitment on how you feel or what your spouse can give to you. You base it on what you've promised to do for this person.

- You're to live in the cycle of family life with this co-laborer God has honored you with. That means working together, laughing together, crying together, worrying together, rejoicing together, getting bone-tired with each other and, finally, resting together. It means you stand beside this other in the full process of family life.

- You must tend the soil of this special person's heart, helping it grow into a vibrant, life-giving garden that blooms with the fullness of "human beingness" that God created.

- Your life as a spouse now mysteriously reflects the beautiful unity of Christ and His church and the sacrificial nature of Christ, who emptied Himself on the cross. This means your marriage is a living proclamation of Christ. You should make sure it's a true proclamation.

We love Christ in our marriages by seeking to make sure our unions reflect these qualities in our daily lives by the power and influence of God's Holy Spirit. Live in it. Seize it. Cherish it.

CHAPTER 6

BEING SOMEONE'S PARENT

God, with all his angels and creatures, is smiling, not because that father is washing diapers, but because he is doing so in Christian faith. Those who sneer at him and see only the task but not the faith are ridiculing God with all his creatures, as the biggest fool on earth. Indeed, they are only ridiculing themselves; with all their cleverness they are nothing but devil's fools.

MARTIN LUTHER, THE ESTATE OF MARRIAGE, 1522

As a husband and the father of a brood of young children, I'll be honest with you: In the midst of my parental day, I sometimes dream of a number of things I would rather be doing right now than living a domestic life. Between doling out innumerable sippy cups freshly stocked with "shoosh" (or "juice," as adults call it), picking up the ubiquitous crayons that litter our kitchen and family room floor, or cleaning bathrooms and changing poopers, I often entertain fantasies of what it'd be like to scream down a winding trail on my mountain bike, read Flannery O'Connor in a quiet and dimly lit café somewhere, or just have long periods free of "Daddy will you . . . ?" for concentration on writing. (And while we're dreaming, why not a week alone with Jackie touring the museums of Amsterdam?) I'm sure you harbor similar dreams.

But lately, I've been powerfully struck by the truth that there is no more substantive, revolutionary task than parenting a child. We tend to think it's politicians, actors, musicians, and writers who hold most of the power. But their influence is minimal compared to a parent's.

Those who are begetting, raising, and molding members of the next generation engage in nothing less than forever changing the balance of the universe and history. The world will be a very different place—for good or bad—because a parent *is* or *is not* parenting a child.

Parenting Children Is a Mirror of . . .

Of all people, Christians should have a view of parenting based on the understanding that the sum of parenting is much bigger than the myriad tasks involved. Christians understand that parenting is a mirror of three things: the father heart of God, God as Creator, and the mystery of the Trinity.

The Father Heart of God

As we explored earlier, God reveals Himself to us as Father. Jesus taught us that the Father is an intimate, loving daddy. Some say the experiences we have with our own father affect the way we see God. If our father was harsh and conditional with us, we'll tend to see God that way. If he was weak and convictionless, we'll understand God as such. If he was gracious but firm, loving, and just, that's the way we'll perceive God.

In a real way, parents stand in the place of God for their children when the kids are young. As they get older, they learn about God for themselves, but that picture remains greatly shaped by their experience with their parents. We have the responsibility to take great care to ensure that the picture we live out before our children demonstrates who God is rather than hindering their image of Him. Our example should bring them closer to knowing and loving Him.

Parenting and the Father

In 1868, George MacDonald wrote in *The Seaboard Parish*, "A parent must respect the spiritual person of his child, and approach it with reverence, for that too looks the Father in the face and has an audience with Him into which no earthly parent can enter even if he dared to desire it."[1]

God as Creator

Nothing comes into being without God the Creator. Yet man and woman uniquely become participants with God when they bring forth new life in creating new persons. This participation with God in creation reminds me of some old poetry from George MacDonald:

Creation thou dost work by faint degrees,
By shade and shadow from unseen beginning;
Far, far apart, in unthought mysteries
Of thy own dark, unfathomable seas,
Thou will'st thy will; and thence, upon the earth—

Slow traveling, his way through centuries winning—
A child at length arrives at never ending birth.[2]

Animals and plants bring forth new life, but only people bring forth new humans who bear the image of God. Parents participate with God in this wonderful creative process, not only as they unite physically, but also as they develop a full-orbed relationship—emotionally, domestically, and willfully—bringing new life out of that fullness. This act happens in an instant yet continues throughout the rest of life.

People can create new life with only the physical part of the relationship (and with the "blessing" of technology, even the physical is no longer necessary). But if that new life is born into a relationship between a man and woman that is only physical, it has difficulty coming to full human maturity. This new life will thrive most richly when its parents reflect the relational qualities of the Trinity: intimacy, love, service, commitment, exclusivity, cooperative interaction, and faithfulness.

The Mystery of the Trinity

As we discussed previously, the trinity of father, mother, and child is the closest picture in creation to the ultimate reality of the Trinity of God. Just as Father, Son, and Holy Spirit are three persons, but all have one essence, so are father, mother, and child. Again, this earthly trinity isn't a perfect picture of the heavenly Trinity. But this family triad is the best picture of God's sacred community because He created family to reflect this.

WHAT MAKES PARENTING SPIRITUAL?

As a Christian, I'm interested in pleasing God. As a Christian parent, I'm interested in discovering what part of my job as a parent is of special interest to God. I must ask, "What does God want from me as a parent?"

Part of the answer to this question is addressed in the points just discussed. We reflect the parental heart of God that is centered in intimacy and that expects holy obedience and faithfulness while tirelessly extending grace when that standard is broken. We're also participants with God in the creative process, not just in bringing new life into the world, but also as God's primary agents in bringing that new life into God's intended fullness. As procreative Christ-ones, our job is to help our children become Christ-ones in the fullest possible way.

Parenting Fully Alive Children

The early church father Irenaeus proclaimed, *Gloria Dei vivens homo:* "the glory of God is man fully alive."[3] A human person fully alive is the glory of God. What does it mean for parents to help God create little human beings that are fully alive?

It means we partner with God in developing the following in our children.

- *Souls,* which are the center of their being and connect them with the transcendent qualities of life. While we're concerned with where their souls will spend eternity, it doesn't end there. We need to be concerned with the quality of their souls today. We cultivate souls like hearty soil that sprouts intimate love for God, a sensitivity to and recognition of His hand working in the world and their lives, and a love for others that matches the love they have for themselves.

- *Intellects* that are well trained to be curious and seek the truth of God found in Scripture and all the wonder of His creation. A book that provides a good vision for this in its fullness is *The Well-Trained Mind: A Guide to Classical Education at Home* by Jessie Wise and Susan Wise Bauer (W.W. Norton & Company, 1999). Check it out at *http://www.welltrainedmind.com/moreabout-book.html*

- *Physical bodies* that are strong, healthy, and well cared for, allowing them to do all the things God has for them in their long, productive lives.

- *Creativity,* one of the obvious characteristics we uniquely share with God. We should teach our children to be as creative as God. They can enjoy and contribute to the beauty of literature, art, home and garden design, music, and drama, while knowing that God is interested in all of this. Edith Schaeffer's book *The Hidden Art* (Tyndale, 1985) is very helpful in this.

- *Sense of humor,* another unique reflection of God in us. If you don't think God has a sense of humor then you must believe that the big rainbow-colored rear end you see on that primate at the zoo or the mouth on that platypus just evolved that way. Our children should know how to laugh appropriately and make others laugh also. I've heard Christians say they wish they could hear the apostle Paul preach. I wish I could hear Jesus laugh. I imagine it's a grand laugh, and it's one of the joys of heaven we'll hear one day.

- *Emotions,* which also reflect the character of God. God isn't emotionally passive. Our children must learn there's a time for anger (and then a time to stop), a time for sadness, and a time for laughter. Our children should be taught sensitivity to and identification with other people's emotions.

We honor God when each of these parts of our God-created humanity blooms in our children. To ignore them is to diminish the most important part of God's creation and therefore ignore the glory of God in the world.

One way we help our children become Christ-ones is by helping them think beyond the things we typically imagine as spiritual, such as regularly attending church and Sunday school, having a daily quiet time, and praying at meals.

Don't get me wrong. These are vitally important disciplines that should be a regular part of family life. But we make a mistake when we think these things are the primary substance of our spiritual lives. These "spiritual" things aren't an end but are important things that feed an end.

So, what *does* God want from parents?

Helping Children Recognize the Fullness of Lordship

God wants us to love Him by bringing His lordship to bear on *all* parts of our lives. He wants us to recognize that we live in our Father's world. It's full of His glory—not just in the splendor of the seas or the majesty of the mountains and forests, but also in the normalness of everyday family life. God's glory shows forth in a job well done, a meal prepared (and cleaned up) well, a yard mowed nicely, a tee-ball team coached with loving care. As Martin Luther explained so long ago, God and the angels smile when a father changes a diaper.

But how can reading *Blueberries for Sal* to my four-year-old daughter or trying to catch a glimpse with my boy of that old Grey owl down by the stream be pleasing to God? They're so normal! The truth is that these simple things bring God glory because His image bearers are participating in the life of His world. When we recognize this grand fact, these simple tasks become acts of worship. (Yes, wiping cream cheese off your two-year-old's face is an act of worship!) These seemingly mundane things of domestic life are part of God's original creation, not products of the Fall, which means they're intrinsically sacred, no matter how normal they seem. Elizabeth Barrett Browning recognized this wonderful fact when she wrote,

> Earth's crammed with heaven,
> And every common bush afire with God:
> But only he who sees, takes off his shoes,
> The rest sit round it and pluck blackberries,
> And daub their natural faces unawares . . . [4]

One of our most important jobs as parents is to teach this truth to our children, helping them understand it and live it out. But how?

First, we teach our children that Christ is Lord over all of life and not just religious life. Put another way, there's not a single part of creation that doesn't have God's intense interest and fascination. After all, He made it and sustains it moment by moment.

What Is God's?

At the dedication service of the Free University in Amsterdam in 1880, founder Abraham Kuyper insisted in his address, "There is not one square inch in the whole domain of our human existence over which Christ, who is sovereign over *all*, does not cry: 'Mine!'"[5]

We're not watering down what it means to be spiritual when we say that all of life—no matter how mundane—is sacred. The very reverse is true. We limit God—the Maker and Sustainer of heaven and earth—when we say that He's only interested in the parts of life we see as expressly religious. How wrong! His interests are as large as His creation.

Second, we help our children see that they honor and love God when they participate in the normalcy of everyday life— when they do it well and glory in the beauty that it all flows from Him. Something is deeply sacred about participating in creation. The difference between Christians and others is that Christians recognize that creation flows from God, rather than being a god. We also recognize that when our Savior became man, He participated in and therefore sanctified these things. To most nonChristians (and unfortunately to many Christians), daily life is just another thing to do to get ready for the weekend.

It's my job to help my children see Christ in all parts of life.

What Does God Command of Parents?

God doesn't give many specific commands directly to parents in Scripture. The most foundational command to parents is in Deuteronomy 6:5-7, where God says, "Love the LORD your God with all your heart and with all your soul and with all your strength. These commandments that I give you today are to be upon your hearts. Impress them on your children. Talk about them when you sit at home and when you walk along the road, when you lie down and when you get up" (NIV).

Parents should love God with every part of their being, model that love for their children, and teach their children the commandments of God. But we don't do this by setting aside some special time of instruction cut off from the rest of life. Rather, we accomplish it as an intentionally integrated part of daily home life. Children should learn from their parents that God's commands mean something in real day-to-day life. Our children learn when they hear it *and* observe it, for the two reinforce one another.

Proverbs 22:6 exhorts parents to "train a child in the way he should go, and when he is old he will not turn from it" (NIV).

Solomon tells us two things here. First, how we train a child today will affect the kind of adult he or she grows into. Second, there *is* a way a child should go. There's a path that's right for a child and another that's wrong. Parents should instruct their children in the path that is right. To do this, we need to be tuned in to how God made our children so we can know the way they should go. We shouldn't train up a child with a particular temperament and passion to be something God didn't make him or her to be.

Another command is for fathers not to "provoke your children to anger; but bring them up in the discipline and instruction of the Lord" (Ephesians 6:4). Elsewhere, Paul warns fathers not to "exasperate your children, that they may not lose heart" (Colossians 3:21). While Paul doesn't address mothers in these verses, I don't think he's giving moms a pass on exasperating their kids; rather, he recognizes that moms don't seem to struggle as much with this tendency. Parents are to be gracious and patient in teaching their children the ways of God in all of life.

Do you think parents don't exasperate their kids? Tonight, while Jackie was out running some errands, I was giving the kids showers and baths. Jackie called to check on us, and while I had her on the phone, I was giving Sophie directions on finishing her shower. Jackie said, "Glenn, give the girl a break; a child can only process so many directions. Let her be." At the same time, Sophie had a look on her face that screamed, "Give me a break; I can only process so many directions. Let me be." Both were right. I was exasperating my child.

Be Intentional

Each of these commands — train our children and don't exasperate them — has something in common with the others that we don't always readily appreciate. The primary idea about parenting in Scripture is that parents should know where they're going in the job of parenting and how they'll get there. (Cheat sheet: This means raising kids who love God, love others, who seek His holiness, and who seek to expand Christ's kingdom in their lives and the world.) Simplified further, parents should be — in a word — *intentional*.

Fewer parents are doing this today.

Several years ago, a television documentary and book came out looking at youth in America, drawing a frightening picture of parents in America. The documentary was done by the Public Broadcasting System, and it was called *The Lost Children of Rockdale County*. It began as a look at a syphilis outbreak in the spring of 1996 in Conyers, Georgia, an affluent suburb of Atlanta. As the crew's investigation unfolded, they found that the heart of the story wasn't the outbreak. It was how more than two hundred upper-middle-class teens contracted the disease.

These kids lived in beautiful homes and had all the material things teenagers could want. But their parents set almost no rules for them. The teens did drugs, drank, and had wild group-sex parties — all under the apathetic gaze of their parents. Some knew their kids were involved in such behavior and just couldn't muster the parental resolve to do anything, or they were just too busy making money for "stuff" to care. The clue-lessness of these well-educated and professionally successful parents was stunning. They showed more intentionality in managing their retirement accounts than their children. The parents almost seemed like good actors playing bone-headed parents; you couldn't imagine real parents being this dense. But they were.

Another picture of parents was presented in a book by Patricia Hersch titled *A Tribe Apart: A Journey into the Heart of American Adolescence.* To research her book, Hersch entered the world of eight "average" middle-class adolescents in a Virginia town and lived among them for three years. She observed that these young people were "a tribe apart," not because they rebelled and separated themselves from the community, but because their parents neglected them—not materially, but parentally. Like the teens of Rockdale County, Georgia, these kids were adrift.

Most troubling is that these children seem to be the norm rather than the exception. More and more children live in urban and suburban versions of *Lord of the Flies:* stranded in their own neighborhoods, exiled from their parents, left to make up their own rules and to live by their self-created social codes. And the lives they're living aren't pretty.

These children are a new breed of orphan. They have bio-logically connected material-providers, but they don't have emo-tionally connected parents. They don't have mothers and fathers who make them feel like they matter. They don't have parents who set protective boundaries or ennobling expectations. They don't have parents who are emotionally nurturing or behav-iorally directive. They don't have parents who strive to richly stock the wardrobe of their moral imaginations or deliberately work to develop the architecture of their characters. They don't have parents who love them with time and intimacy, rather than merely with stuff. They don't have parents who *parent,* for these are the primary deeds of parents.

Children need parents who are crazy about them, parents who get involved in their lives on a daily basis—when it's easy and when it's hard. Parents are participants with God in creating and maturing new human beings. They should be intentional about the kinds of human beings they're helping God produce.

Parents should have good answers to the following questions:

- What do I want my child to understand about God?
- What do I want my child to believe about himself or herself?
- What personal qualities do I want my child to value most highly?
- How does my child know I believe in and love him or her?
- Does my child get that message?
- Do I love my child by giving him or her my time?
- Do I teach my child by example what it means to love Christ in daily life?
- How do I want my child to view work? How am I teaching that and is he or she getting it?
- What kinds of books do I want to expose my child to (from the earliest ages)?
- What do I want my child to know about the purpose of life?
- Does my child know what does or does not disappoint me about his or her performance or behavior?

(And parent, you must ask if these are fair and worthy expectations.)

- Does my child know what's most important to me?

Some parenting books try to provide answers to questions like these. But children aren't sugar cookies cut into perfect shapes with a mold. Each one is shaped by God's hand, and He makes you the assistant baker, so you have to answer these questions for yourself.

While books can be helpful, a great way to help develop your own answers to these questions is to talk with the parents around you whom you respect for the job they are doing with their children. Have your Sunday school class, Bible study, or book or play group discuss those questions sometime, and make notes on what you learn.

WHICH PARENTING STYLE DO YOU USE?

Parenting isn't easy. Layered on your child's own break-the-mold individuality is your parenting style (and possibly your spouse's conflicting parenting style). For simplicity, we can break down parenting styles into four main types. Which one do you use in raising your child?

Authoritarian Parents

These parents are high on control and rules and low on warmth and emotional interaction with their children. Authoritarian parenting is likely to produce obedient children as long as parents are around. However, when these children are out of their parent's sight, they often engage in reckless behavior; they haven't been allowed to absorb a moral code from their parents, but have had one externally forced upon them. When the opportunity presents itself in later adolescence or early adulthood, they run from this oppression like mice from a cage. Too often, they run into danger.

Buddy Parents

These parents are high on warmth and low on control and rules. They're more like peers than parents. Adolescents from these homes often perceive themselves as equals who don't need to listen to adults. Rather than actually becoming buddies, these children grow to resent their parents for not being parents. Unfortunately, this pattern is represented by a growing number of parents, and their children are growing up with remarkable issues of insecurity, anger, lack of moral code, and lack of direction.

Laissez-Faire Parents

These parents—being low on warmth *and* low on control—are the extreme of nonparents. They let kids make their own rules and offer no correction in the face of troubling behavior and they show no real emotional concern for their children. Obviously, this is not good. Often these kids become very assertive because they realize they have to be. Their parents aren't going to make a way for them. But this assertiveness is typically very antisocial, expressed in gang violence for boys and in early child-bearing for girls. Their parents don't affirm them, so they have to tell the world they matter. Guns and babies are how they do it.

Authoritative Parents

High levels of both emotional warmth and disciplinary direction mark this style of parenting. A study reported in the *Journal of the American Medical Association* indicates that this parenting style is the most effective deterrent to adolescent risk behavior, even above the mere presence of a parent in the home at key times.[6] These kids develop two important things that they take with them into their later years. One is the security of knowing that they're loved and someone cares about what they do. The other is that the children develop an internal moral compass that they carry with them at all times, because their parents haven't rigidly forced a long list of rules, but rather have consistently trained their children in some nonnegotiable general principles and helped them understand why those matter.

This last style most closely reflects the character of God, who expects that we live holy and obedient lives and extends endless and loving grace when we blow it.

ALLOWING YOUR KIDS TO FOLLOW CHRIST IN THEIR WAY

As we've discussed earlier, spiritual success isn't a formula. Just as we can't let others determine how we should develop and live out our own love for Christ, we can't determine that for our children.

"But hey, isn't that what parents do?" you might ask. Well, yes and no. God instructs parents to teach and model for their children the things of God. It's their most important task. It's part of the essence of loving Christ in your family. But just as God has given your child a unique set of fingerprints, He's given your child a unique personality and spirit. As your child grows and develops a relationship with Christ, he or she will become more and more independent of you. That means two things:

1. Your child will start getting his or her own direction from Christ.
2. This may be different from the direction Christ is giving you.

Your responsibility, then, isn't to change the direction to the one you think your children should be going. Rather, it's to make sure they're hearing God well. Of course, this can be difficult to discern—for both children and parents. The first step is determining whether or not the direction they're going lines up generally with Scripture. If it doesn't, you have a responsibility to intervene and help your children discern God's call for themselves in light of God's Word and under the guidance of the Holy Spirit.

However, even if their direction *does* line up with Scripture, that doesn't necessarily mean it's God's will. Now you need to ask other questions like, "Does this seem to fit with my child's gifting, temperament, or style?"

Determining God's Will

Dr. James Dobson, founder and president of Focus on the Family, offers some helpful direction for families in discerning the will of God for their family. He explains these came from a booklet titled *Impression,* written in 1892 by Martin Wells Knapp. Dobson says that God's will for us and our children will always be the following:

Scriptural. God's leading will always be in harmony with Scripture and not just a few select verses here and there. Many things can be justified by picking one or two isolated passages. But we need to test individual parts of Scripture against the truth and continuity of the whole of God's Word.

Right. God will never call us to do what is not right. For example, it's never God's will for us to start a sexual relationship with someone we're not married to or to divorce our spouse and marry someone who "can help us serve God better."

Providential. If the Holy Spirit is leading us in a certain direction, God will open the way for us. When it seems we have to make the way for something because it's just not coming together, it's a good sign God isn't in it. Of course, God's leading isn't always easy, but we don't have to manipulate reality to make it work. God will always make a way for us to obey His will.

Reasonable. God created and reigns over a reasonable world. He'll never ask us to do silly or absurd things that fly in the face of good judgment and common sense. Yes, saints of God in the past have lost their lives because they have followed God's will. But this happened, not because they were doing silly things, but because they were serving God faithfully.

You've probably seen parents who don't take this extra step, pushing their children down a ministry or career path that may fit the parents, but not the children. For example, maybe you have a deep passion for and effective ministry in teaching your church community how to pray strategically for world missions. In fact, you believe in it so much you think everyone else should have this as their central mission. But your child is developing a heart for the people with needs in your community and wants to start a book drive for kids who don't have ready access to books. Do you force your child into your mold or help him or her grow into God's mold? Let your child develop into the one God is developing and has called you to help nurture.

Remember, spiritual success isn't a cookie-cutter formula, but is as vast as God Himself, as expansive as His kingdom, and as diverse as the humanity He created. As a parent, your job is to help your child follow what God has for him or her, not what God has for you. Give your kids the essentials, and glory in how they live them out as the individuals God made them to be.

Raising a Child with an Unbelieving Spouse

Raising children to be what God is calling them to be is tough enough. It can become more difficult when we share the task with a spouse who doesn't share our faith. Most times, unbelieving parents aren't hostile but are indifferent about the spiritual nurturing of their children. And sometimes the experience of seeing children develop a love for Christ can do a great deal to stimulate an unbelieving parent's own spiritual journey.

So, how do you parent children if you have an unbelieving spouse?

- Talk with your spouse about how important it is for your children to have a belief system that answers the most central questions about themselves, about the world, and about the purpose behind it all.

- Encourage your spouse, at the very least, not to hinder or thwart your efforts to raise your children to love Christ. Beyond support and encouragement, ask for your spouse's advice in this task. Inviting your spouse to be a participant in the process can communicate his or her responsibility in this vital job. If your spouse can't actively support you, at least agree on a position of neutrality. This isn't ideal, but it is better for your children than hostility.

- Talk together about how, together, you'll answer the questions, "Why doesn't Mommy go to church with us?" "Why doesn't Daddy pray to Jesus?" or even harder, "Will Momma be in heaven with us?" These are questions that you have to answer honestly but age-appropriately. It's best to determine together what your common answer will be so your children don't hear conflicting messages.

This process, pursued lovingly and prayerfully, can serve to help foster your unbelieving spouse's own spiritual understanding. It's amazing what can happen in the heart of a parent when his or her child's well-being is at stake. Remember, few people get nagged into the kingdom. Most come because someone loved them in the name of Christ—because someone prayed for them and graciously told them why they need Christ and how they can become His children.

Renewing Your Energy

As Jackie and I fall into bed every night, worn out from the day of caring for five active children, we find refreshment and renewed energy when we remind each other that we are collaborators with God in the wonderful and sacred work of creating new life and bringing that life to full maturity. Our role as parents calls us to lovingly and intentionally guide our children toward becoming people who love God and enjoy Him forever. And we are to help them do this as the glorious individuals God made them to be, with the skills and passions He gives them. We can start businesses, write books, build houses, teach classes, establish ministries. But no job—no matter how grand—can outweigh the importance of parenting a child. Parents, more than anyone else, shape tomorrow by shaping children today.

In 1522, Martin Luther wrote in *The Estate of Marriage,*

Alas, must I rock the baby, wash its diapers, make its bed, smell its stench, stay up nights with it, take care of it when it cries, heal its rashes and sores . . . take care of this and take care of that, do this and do that, endure this and endure that, and whatever else of bitterness and drudgery married life involves?

What then does Christian faith say to this? It opens its eyes, looks upon all these insignificant, distasteful, and despised duties in the Spirit, and is aware that they are all adorned with divine approval as with the costliest gold and jewels. It says, "O God, because I am certain that thou hast created me . . . and hast from my body begotten this child, I also know for a certainty that it meets with thy perfect pleasure. I confess to thee that I am not worthy to rock the little babe or wash its diapers . . . or to be entrusted with the care of the child. How is it that I, without any merit, have come to this distinction of being certain that I am serving thy creature and thy most precious will? O how gladly will I do so . . . for I am certain that it is thus pleasing in thy sight.[7]

Be engaged. Be intentional. Seize it.

CHAPTER 7

BEING SOMEONE'S CHILD

Your Savior and the Lord of all creation is Someone's
Child.

I am sitting here on a Saturday morning quietly watching my lovely eight-year-old daughter fix breakfast for herself and her sleepover friend. I hardly recognize my own little girl. In this moment I appreciate and marvel at how quickly she has grown and what an amazing person she's becoming. I marvel at this in all my children. How each slow, plodding day has somehow made up years that have just whizzed by. When did she become such a beautiful young girl who interacts so confidently and maturely with her friend? She is so much more confident than I ever was as a child. I realize the process of her childhood has been a glorious and beautiful thing.

Contrast this with what I saw in a very powerful film I viewed last weekend. What made this film so engaging? It wasn't the special effects. There were none. It wasn't the exciting characters. They weren't spectacular or larger than life. It wasn't even the music in the movie, which can so powerfully drive the emotions. The power was found in the story itself, because it demonstrated the importance of childhood, connectedness, and family.

The film, *Antwone Fisher,* is a true story about a young black man having trouble keeping his career as a Navy seaman on track. The rage within his soul drives him to fight anyone who crosses him in the slightest way. Of course, the Navy doesn't tolerate this behavior, and they send him to a psychiatrist to straighten him out.

His relationship with the counselor grows as they establish trust with each other. We find Antwone's problems rooted in the fact that he was robbed of his childhood. He was born in prison to a mother who never bothered to find him when she got out. His father was violently killed shortly afterward as a consequence of an affair. A mean and violent foster mom raised him. Her daughter sexually molested him regularly. He was never allowed the innocence of childhood, and he raged at a world that denied him this. ˙

In the midst of his therapy, this angry but thoughtful young man reads one of his poems to his therapist. Every line asks, "Who will cry for the little boy?" Antwone is asking the world, "Who will weep with me that I never had the chance to be loved, cared for, allowed to be a little boy, and taught how to be a man?" The last line of the poem declares, "I will cry—I always do." He's been the only one who can console himself. No one has been there for him.

The message I got from this film is that the innocence of childhood matters profoundly and that childhood is about living closely with others in the warmth and love of family. This is no surprise for Christians. It is no small thing that at the center of the Christian story is Someone's Child, the only Son of the Father and the offspring of Mary, an earthly mother. As you ponder your own role as someone's child, with all the good and all the bad, it's significant to remember that your Savior and the Lord of all creation is and has been Someone's Child from eternity. God became a human child in Christ and grew through all the stages of childhood into the teen years and young adulthood. He's not a God who can't relate to your life and experiences as a child. To answer Antwone's question, it is Christ who cries for the child. He weeps at the loss of innocence. He gave Himself to win it back.

In fact, one of the most important things novelist George MacDonald learned from his father was that fatherhood and sonship are the core of the universe.[1] And as we recall how everything began—with a Triune Creator God—we see that MacDonald's father is right. The relationship between the Parent and Child (with the Holy Spirit) is the fount of all existence and reality. You should realize you mirror this ultimate and glorious reality as you live out your family role as a son or daughter. As a parent, your life with your child is a unique clarion call to each generation and every community of what God is like. That's a lot to understand and fully appreciate because it's such a huge truth.

The Implications of Fatherhood

Over the next few days and weeks, think about why it matters for you as a family member that everything that *is* flows out of a relationship between a Father and a Child. Don't try to answer the question too quickly, because this is a big question with a wealth of implications.

What's Required of a Child?

Christ is very clear about what He expects of us. He commands us to love God with everything we have and every part of our being. In addition, we're to love everyone around us as we love ourselves. Adherence to these two laws is the most significant sign of how a child (and we're *all* someone's child) is pleasing to God. C. S. Lewis said that our spiritual health is directly proportionate to our love for God.[2] And teach your child what Pascal taught us: "What a long way it is between knowing God and loving Him!"[3]

A more specific requirement of children is found in Ephesians and Colossians, where Christ commands children to obey their parents. This simple command includes a grand promise. Obeying your parents pleases the Lord and leads to a long, good life. By obeying our parents, we model the behavior and attitude of the Son who said, "For I have come down from heaven, not to do My own will, but the will of Him who sent Me" (John 6:38). Jesus obeyed His Father in everything He was instructed to do, even when He preferred not to, as when He struggled to the point of sweating blood on the eve of going to the cross (see Matthew 26:38-39; Luke 22:44).

Our children must learn to understand and accept God's point of view. Obeying their parents is simple and nonnegotiable. They should just do it. And when they do, they win God's favor and avoid all kinds of bad stuff.

What Children Must Do

> Children, be obedient to your parents in all things, for this is well-pleasing to the Lord. (Colossians 3:20)

> Children, obey your parents in the Lord, for this is right. HONOR YOUR FATHER AND MOTHER (which is the first commandment with a promise), THAT IT MAY BE WELL WITH YOU, AND THAT YOU MAY LIVE LONG ON THE EARTH. (Ephesians 6:1-3)

We've had to drive this truth home to a few of our kids in a powerful way recently. They were going through a time when it seemed they didn't think they needed to obey us. When we'd correct them, they'd ignore us and continue doing whatever they were doing. What brazen boldness!

They needed to understand that obeying wasn't optional and failing to do so could have serious consequences, both in punishment from us and from the natural consequences of their behavior. Desperate, Jackie got a flash of wisdom and decided to bring out the big guns and use a powerful illustration from a sobering discussion we'd all had the day before.

That day, on our way to the store, we had seen something new on a telephone pole and the kids asked about it. It was a white cross and some flowers fashioned into a memorial marking an event well known in our area from the media. A teenage girl had sneaked out of her house late one night and gone joyriding with her boyfriend. He'd been drinking, and when his car struck that utility pole at high speed, she was killed instantly.

Jackie asked our daughters to remember the cross and flowers we'd seen. She told them how this young girl's parents thought she was upstairs asleep in her bed, safe and sound, when they got the call from the police that shattered their world. The girl knew her parents wouldn't allow her to go out late at night with her friend because they knew it wasn't safe. Maybe she didn't understand that and she probably thought it was unfair. "But her parents knew what was best for her," Jackie told the girls. And then she explained, ready to hit the nail hard, "If she had obeyed her parents, she'd still be here today, and her parents and family wouldn't be so sad right now! But instead, she disobeyed her parents and now she's gone and her whole family and all her friends are very sad." Of course, we assured them that acts of disobedience seldom end so tragically, but some can.

We also told them that all acts of disobedience have *some* consequences. Some we realize immediately. Others we don't. But each one grieves the heart of God, and that's something a Christian never wants to do. Most important, obedience is an act and expression of love. Jesus obeyed His Father because of the love they shared. In families, it's something we do to honor another. Spouses obey one another because of love. Children should obey their parents from love. And love compels parents to obey God in the task of parenting their children well. Obedience is a demonstration of love. Disobedience is not.

WHAT ABOUT OBEYING PARENTS WHO DON'T BELIEVE?

What if your children have a parent who doesn't love God or seek to serve Him? Do they still need to obey?

In a word, *yes*.

The commands found in Colossians and Ephesians don't add a qualifier about obeying only believing parents or parents who are always kind. There's no statute of limitations either. However, we do know that when we marry, we leave mother and father and cleave to our spouse. This means we seek to please our spouse before all others.

But what if a parent demands that his or her children do things contrary to God's direction or forbids them from doing things God calls them to? Generally, it's a rare parent who'd discourage a child from developing an obedient and loving relationship with God. This isn't love on the part of a parent.

Here's what you teach your children if there's a possibility they might face this situation: you must obey God. You must obey God in what He is calling you to do, and you must, to the best of your ability, honor your parents. If a conflict arises and it's difficult to determine what to do, seek the counsel of the believing parent or the direction of an older believer you trust. It would be particularly helpful if this person knows both parent and child. This older, wiser believer can help you understand what God is calling you to do, whether it's correct, and how to help your parents understand it. Of course, this person might also help you understand why parents would say no and why it's really wise that they do. As Proverbs 13:10 says, "Through presumption comes nothing but strife. But with those who receive counsel is wisdom."

If it turns out that obeying God conflicts with obeying a parent, your child needs to seek to honor the parent as much as possible. Children can learn to explain to this parent their desire to obey because God commands it, but also that the parent must not hinder their desire to follow God's direction. Disagreeing with parents can still be done with much prayer, with guidance from older Christians, and with love and respect.

I had this struggle when I was a teenager. At seventeen, I was drawn into a church tradition much different from the one I was raised in. This concerned my parents greatly, for they weren't at all familiar with the kind of church I was going to.

My parents had their church leaders talk to me about my decisions. I had to honor my parents' concern, but I also had to show them why I was making this decision and how I was actually seeking to live out the things they and God had taught me, in a way that was right for me. My parents wisely gave me room while at the same time kept a close eye on me.

Can You Be a Teenager and Be a Christian?

Parents and teens both ask this question, because the teen years can be such a tumultuous ride of increasing hormones, racing emotions, and developing bodies. In many ways, the teen years are humanity in transition and therefore humanity out of control. Dr. Dobson has aptly described the teen years as a stretch of mountain river that develops Class 4 rapids for a few miles. It gets pretty bumpy and sometimes it seems as if you might flip and lose everything. But eventually you get past the rough patch and you return to a more peaceful adventure. The experience of most parents and teens says he's right.

I wonder how many adolescents struggle with the question of being a Christian and a teenager. I suppose more than we imagine. When I was a teen I wanted to serve and love God but found it very difficult to do. The difficulty wasn't so much due to persecution from friends, but came from struggles on the inside. I was a raging bundle of passions. I wanted to do a bunch of stuff; some of it I wanted to do real bad and some of it *was* real bad. Often I had a very hard time controlling my behavior and my attitude. Thankfully, God protected me from myself.

I wrote earlier about spouting off to my mom and getting slapped in the face for it. When she hit me, I laughed at her. All the while I was seeking to serve and please Christ, but I could be so mean. In many ways I was out of control. It was as if, like the apostle Paul described in Romans 7, I desired to do one thing, but I watched another person (me) do exactly the opposite. I was a mess. How could I be a Christian?

Are your teens like I was? Deep inside they seem to ask themselves, "How can I honor Christ and hold it all together when it seems everything is flying apart?" There are some answers to this question.

First, they grow out of it. They simply mature. They learn to temper their emotions and desires. They mature in their faith. Your child might meet someone who will help him or her mature and become more cultured and civilized. I met Jackie when I was seventeen, and this is one of the great things she did for me.

Second, they learn to live under the influence. As Christians, we have the third person of the Trinity dwelling within us and seeking to flow out of us. Let the Holy Spirit do what He's there to do in your teen. He's the one who convicts us of sin when we do wrong (see John 16:8). And His residence in our soul, body, and life produces righteousness like fruit that grows from a vine (see Galatians 5:22-23). Encourage your teen to yield to the Spirit's power and influence.

Third, they learn to confess and repent. When we blow it—and we all do—we must come clean with our sin before God and repent. God knows our sin anyway, but He wants us to be honest before Him about it. Help your teen to understand that repenting means being broken about your sin *and* having a change of mind and will *and* seeking forgiveness. Repentance comes from God, as the Holy Spirit works within us to transform us into what God desires us to be.

Fourth, they learn to be accountable to others. There are no lone rangers in the kingdom of God. It's a community. God places all of us—including your teenager—in community with others (in church as well as in the world) and that community is a God-given gift to help keep us on the path via accountability, encouragement, prayer, and confession.

Dietrich Bonhoeffer, a Lutheran pastor who was executed in a Nazi concentration camp, uniquely understood the gift of community. His lonely prison cell helped him appreciate a profound truth: "It is easily forgotten that the fellowship of Christian brethren is a gift of grace, a gift of the Kingdom of God that any day may be taken from us."[4]

The teen years aren't easy years for the Christian family to navigate and certainly aren't years when it's easy for parents to remain strong in their faith. But God hasn't left us to work the whole thing out by ourselves. God gives each family great help in the Holy Spirit and the community of believers.

BECOMING YOUR OWN PERSON IN YOUNG ADULTHOOD

As we discussed early in this book, Christian discipleship and spirituality isn't practiced in just one way. There's no one-size-fits-all Christian life—contrary to what some Christian teachers would tell us. As Christ encountered people, He met and interacted with each as an individual. While Scripture provides general principles and commands common to all of us, there are as many ways of living those out as there are people. God made me different from you and we will both obey the commands to care for the orphans and widows or pray for our elected public officials in different ways.

As parents, we're obedient to and honor Christ when we raise our children to be the people He created them to be. Help your children discover new things about God and the life He has for them. Help them build confidence to follow the way God has for them and become the person He is calling them to be. Help them learn to hear from God for themselves. Help them find great mentors. Help them obey God's command to love Him and others, and to obey and honor their parents. Help them understand they have the help of Christ's redemptive work and the Holy Spirit's power to keep them on track.

My Spiritual Mentors

For what it's worth, here are some spiritual mentors who have influenced me over the years through books and life example:

Francis A. Schaeffer: Schaeffer, more than anyone, helped me develop a spirituality that did three essential things:

- See the lordship of Christ over "all of Life and all of life equally," as Schaeffer often put it.
- Realize that love is the mark of the Christian.
- Know that all people matter, should be taken seriously, and should be treated with dignity.

G. K. Chesterton: He turned my understanding of Christian family life on its head.

Karol Wojtyla: A Polish Catholic priest and philosopher who later became Pope John Paul II, he was one of the most consequential figures of the twentieth century and I encourage you to read about him and find out why I say that. He helped me understand that all of creation holds together under the lordship of the incarnate Christ. As a result, I see that Christianity is a very sophisticated faith and belief system, providing meaningful answers to humanity's deepest questions and reasons for our strongest yearnings in ways far more profound than I ever imagined. He has helped me understand how fully true and beautiful Christianity is.

C. S. Lewis: He's done much to help me think critically on the most important questions. He has no medium thoughts. Besides, he is just a delight to read. His life example is that he was usually gracious, possessed a fierce sense of humor, and lived large parts of his life completely for others.

CHAPTER 8

MYTHS OF A CHRISTIAN FAMILY

*Let times change, let the weather change, but do not
invent an adulterated family and drink from it as if it
were the real nourishing thing.*

ALVARO DE SILVA, BRAVE NEW FAMILY

*There are no rules of architecture for a castle in the
clouds.*

G. K. CHESTERTON, THE EVERLASTING MAN

I don't know where I got the idea, but as a child I believed that
if I followed some absolute script or order to life, it would lead
to a life that worked out just right all the time. As a boy, I was to
discern and follow this script that was largely set by the author-
ity figures in my life. If a teacher or Scout leader took me to a
room, sat me down in a chair, and told me to sit there until they
came to get me, they could come back four hours later and I
would be sitting right there where they left me. I figured that was
the role I was to play, and if I did, everything would work out
with my world.

I somehow imagined that everyone did the same thing. They
followed their script. My parents did. When my mother took me
to the doctor for an illness, I presumed the doctor would do
exactly what his doctor script called for and I'd be fine. Following

the script is what each one of us did and because we did, life always worked out.

My young life was unscarred by any tragedy. No one I loved died suddenly. My father never lost his job, and he always came home from work on time. I lived a pretty orderly life. I assumed life would stay this way if we all followed our script.

Jackie didn't understand life this way at all. Losing her dad to a heart attack at an early age, she grew up with the dramatic realization that life can change radically at any moment for no particular reason. She grew up in reality. I grew up believing in a myth.

What is a myth? *Webster's Seventh New Collegiate Dictionary* describes a myth as "an ill-founded belief held uncritically, especially by an interested group." Anthropologists help us understand that cultures and civilizations throughout human history construct myths and stories that help them make sense of their world and provide meaning, structure, and context to their lives. Christ spent a good bit of time challenging the myths held by those around Him: the rich young ruler, the Pharisees, Judas, Peter, and others who held various ideas about winning favor with God or why Christ had come. Christians still create myths to help them deal with life, and many of these affect how we view and live in family relationships.

While I'll address some myths here, I'll only scratch the surface. As you explore these, try thinking on your own and with family or friends about additional myths Christians might hold about family. Be sure to think not only about the myths other people hold, but also about the ones you might hold. Then think about the truths that should replace these myths.

THE SOUL MATE MYTH:
"GOD HAS A SPOUSE WHO'S PERFECT FOR ME"

People who aren't married usually hold this view. Those who are married, no matter how wonderful the spouse and marriage, know better.

This myth is the idea that God has a perfect soul mate for each of us and our task is to find that one person who will fit us like a hand in a glove. This isn't how God works it.

This highly romanticized view of marriage is relatively new, springing forth in the past hundred years or so of human history. Earlier, marriage was largely a biologically and economically productive institution, founded primarily on the ideal of what the couple could produce together in terms of offspring, crops, livestock, real materials, and the continuation of family heritage. Physical or emotional attraction sometimes played a role, but it wasn't primary.

My daughters love the *Sarah, Plain and Tall* trilogy, a wonderful story of a widower left to raise two small children and work a small farmstead on the 1900s Kansas prairie. Needing help and companionship, the widower places a newspaper ad for a bride. Sarah, a young and spirited woman from the coast of Maine looking for a new life, answers his ad and moves to Kansas for a month's trial. Initially she dislikes Jacob, but she grows to deeply love him, his children, the animals, and the land. They marry and have a child of their own. Many families were formed this way in days past, and they produced strong, vibrant, loving families.

Yet the soul mate myth stems from a relatively new and romanticized view of marriage and relationships. It's the result of a modern, consumer-driven culture that judges relationships more by their ability to meet our needs and fulfill us than by their ability to act as opportunities to give of ourselves and invest in the lives of others. There are three primary problems with the myth of the perfect spouse.

One: It misunderstands the nature of humanity. Garrison Keillor, in one of his Lake Wobegon tales, said that people who believe in the perfectibility of people only believe that about people they met last Tuesday. Every one of us is marked by original sin. We're seriously flawed and in desperate need of redemption and ongoing sanctification. We bring these flaws into marriage, and our spouses have to live with the reality of them.

Two: This myth fails to appreciate the nature and dynamic of family and marriage in our sanctification. Marriage does many things. Sociologically, it regulates sexual behavior and expression. Biologically, it ensures that both of the adults who have a stake in this new life will raise children from birth to early adulthood, bringing essential and unique contributions to the task of parenting. Theologically, marriage is an icon of the inner life of the Trinitarian God and God's relationship with His people. Psychologically, marriage ideally changes and transforms us into people who are better than we would be without marriage.

Like nothing else, marriage knocks the rough edges off us. Our spouses and children make demands of us, both directly and indirectly requesting that we change our behaviors, attitudes, and desires.

I'm a much better person today than I was twenty years ago because my wife and children demand that I be someone other than I often want to be. People depend on me. I must watch my language because little ears are listening. I must put my things away because I live in a house with others I care about. I must do things I don't want to do, because I want to serve those I love. I can't be selfish, because I get called on it quickly. Christ is redeeming me through these people I call family.

God uses the work, joy, demands, and struggles of marriage as tools to mold us into people who live for others. In this we find contentment and happiness with a richness that can't be found by seeking it directly. If our spouses were just perfect for us, this sanctification wouldn't happen.

Three: The myth of the perfect spouse misunderstands the nature of love. Our wedding vows are founded on the understanding that love, dedication, and commitment won't automatically flow from our heart every day. If they did, we wouldn't need to promise them. Promises are only necessary when we're likely to fail. Without another person who demands our charity and sacrifice by their imperfections, love can't be everything Paul defined it to be in 1 Corinthians 13: "Love is patient. . . . It is not rude . . . it is not easily angered, it keeps no record of wrongs. . . . Love . . . always perseveres" (verses 4-7, NIV). Love anticipates and responds to imperfection with matchless grace.

Chesterton helps us understand how perfect imperfection is when he says, "Many a man has been lucky in marrying the woman he loves. But he is luckier in loving the woman he marries."[1]

Soul Mate Reality

In the Christian ideal, one doesn't find a perfect soul mate to enter marriage with, because none exists ready-made. We become soul mates to our betrothed by giving of ourselves without expecting to be repaid over the glorious highs and lows of a lifetime. As Graham Greene said, "A happy marriage is a thing of slow growth."[2]

Stones That Build the Fortress of Marriage

In his *Early Notebooks*, G. K. Chesterton wrote, "Of all human institutions, marriage is the one which most depends upon slow development, upon patience, upon long reaches of times, upon magnanimous compromise, upon kindly habit."[3]

The Happiness Myth:
"God Wants Me to Seek to Be Happy"

This myth is just as wayward as its opposite twin: "God doesn't want me to be happy; He wants me to be faithful."

The central question would be, "Is God's scheme for marriage and family life all about making us happy?" In our Bible study groups we will declare "no" with a bit of spiritual pride because our understanding of happiness is that it is superficial and self-serving—two things that are antithetical to Christian ideals. The good soldier for Christ has nothing to do with self-serving things, right?

But can happiness really be something God is opposed to?

A truly Christian view demands a higher understanding. How can we really think that God opposes happiness? As marriage and family mirror the Trinitarian community from which everything flows, we certainly know this community shares and receives immense (any adjective here is woefully inadequate!) happiness in their communion with one another. As our marriages mirror this community, how can happiness *not* be a part of that?

But here's the key: The happiness that the persons of the Trinity share isn't something they seek. Instead, it's the beautiful fruit of their self-giving love for the Others and their collective interaction with creation. It's an unavoidable by-product of their being, rather than something they pursue.

Likewise, think about the intense wishes we have for our own children. As we give our children away at their weddings, isn't our primary wish for them that they build a long, happy life with their new spouse? Can that desire be much different from our Father's for us?

As we discussed earlier, it is no wonder social scientists have found for decades that married people report being happier and more content in their relationships, sexually and emotionally, than people who are desperately seeking happiness by hopping from relationship to relationship. We benefit when we give ourselves away to others and seek their good over our own. A basic principle of God's kingdom is that we find our lives when we give them away, and we lose our lives when we seek them (see Matthew 10:39; 16:25; Luke 9:24).

Happiness Reality

Happiness is an essential quality of the Christian home because God is supremely happy. But we can't arrive at happiness when we drive straight for it. Happiness is a curious and elusive thing. Those who seek it directly seldom find it, yet it's abundant among those who seek to increase the happiness and joy of others. In marriage and family, happiness isn't the goal, but rather a beautiful, resulting fruit.

"No Fight" Myth:
"We Have a Great Marriage Because We Never Fight"

Jackie and I know a couple from college who've spoken proudly that they've never had a serious argument in their many years of marriage. When I hear this, I'm tempted to take their pulse to see if they're alive. How can two people live together, day in and day out, and never have a serious argument?

The absence of conflict isn't necessarily a sign of a great marriage or relational virtue, but usually an indication that these people are either soulless beings or they don't know how to express themselves. I'll admit that two people *can* simply have very mild, compliant temperaments, but this is a mark of their personalities rather than the quality of their marriage.

Typically, if you put two people together for any length of time, they're going to disagree. This is especially true if they're married and working to establish a home. In the couple I mentioned previously, she's as hard-driving as a tornado and he's stunningly passive. The reason they never have any arguments is because he never challenges her.

Of course, couples that argue incessantly don't necessarily have a good marriage either. But the sign of a good marriage isn't the absence of conflict or even low levels of conflict, necessarily; rather, it's how the couple handles their conflicts. Do they resolve them fairly and respectfully? Do they know how to bring their disagreements to peaceful resolution, rather than throwing gas on it and inciting it to an emotional, physical, or verbal inferno?

Fight, Fight!

George Bernard Shaw said, "The test of a [couple's] breeding is how they behave in a quarrel."[4]

The beauty of relationship is that we always face the opportunity and possibility of great passion — and passion is a two-way street. Sometimes this passion is desirable, beautiful, and glorious. Other times, the passion is of another nature and very undesirable. Either way, you're messing with fire and the consequences can be spectacular, in every possible meaning of the word. Little human babies can spring forth from one kind of passion, but nasty relational pus can ooze from the other. A healthy relationship will likely have both kinds of passion, with the former outweighing the latter in frequency and intensity.

"No Fight" Reality

Without problems and conflict in a marriage, we don't have any need for love, grace, forgiveness, and reconciliation. Nor do we really have a need for Christ. Perhaps St. Jerome is a tad cynical, but he communicated more truth than falsehood when he said, "He who is not arguing is not married."[5]

Baby Steppin' Myth: "If We Pray, Read Our Bibles, and Tithe, Everything Will Be Fine"

This myth reminds me of a wonderful scene in the very fun movie *What About Bob?* The main character, Bob (Bill Murray), is a highly neurotic, obsessive-compulsive man who doesn't think he'll be able to survive without his therapist being close by at all times. Bob's new therapist, Dr. Leo Marvin (Richard Dreyfus), puts him on a trendy new therapy program he created called Baby Steps. Dr. Marvin has Bob read his new, best-selling book and follow its ingeniously simple directions: baby step through your problems. Bob becomes a faithful, diligent disciple. But it's not long before Bob's protesting that even though he is following the program to the letter, it's not working because he still has problems. He cries out in desperation to Dr. Marvin, "I'm doing the work! I'm baby-steppin'. I'm not a slacker!"

Some Christians are like Bob, believing that if they do the work of living the outward things they think Christians are supposed to do, family life will fit together like a puzzle. Their kids will be ideal, marriage will be glorious, careers will soar, and the crab-grass problem will disappear.

Healthy, growing Christians spend time reading and drinking up God's Word. They're part of a community of believers. They pray and seek God. But our expectation is faulty if we think by doing these things we'll avoid hardship, failure, or setback. Remember, we don't see any perfect families in Scripture. In fact, most of them are found at the other end of the spectrum. The end of the Christian family is not perfection, but seeing Christ's love, grace, and lordship revealed in daily lives.

Look at David

David is known as "a man after God's own heart." Read the Psalms. They reflect a deep communion with, understanding of, and passion for God. While he was a man of great triumphs, he was also a man of staggering moral failures—probably far more than you will ever experience. There's no such thing as a trial-free life. Even Christ didn't have one. It's a myth.

Baby Steppin' Reality

The spiritual disciplines aren't a means of escaping trials and tribulation in family or any other part of life. However, they are a means of communing with Christ and therefore being able to show the grace and peace of Christ in the midst of the troubles and disappointments life brings. Faithful Christians aren't immune to hardships, but they do have the means to show hope in the midst of their trials.

LOVE HAS DIED MYTH:
"I JUST DON'T LOVE YOU ANYMORE"

We've all heard stories about how the divorce rate is higher among some Christian denominations than among the general population, even atheists and agnostics. Some say this is because atheists and agnostics aren't inclined to get married and therefore are unlikely to divorce. Nice try, but no cigar. It's a fact: Christians in certain denominations do have remarkably high divorce rates.

The Christian Divorce Rate

Barna Research Group found that professing Christians have at least moderately higher divorce rates than the general population, including atheists and agnostics. Twenty-seven percent of those describing themselves as "born-again Christians" are currently or have previously been divorced, compared to 24 percent of the general population.

Baptists and nondenominational Protestant churches (which dominate the Bible Belt) included more adults who'd been divorced (29 percent and 35 percent respectively) than any other Christian group, mainline or otherwise. Lutherans and Catholics had the lowest divorce rates at 21 percent. The rate among atheists and agnostics was also just 21 percent.[6]

But there is good news. Additional research shows that persons who attend church at least weekly are 40 percent less likely to have their relationship break up than those who don't.[7] Perhaps this particular statistic means that calling yourself a Christian doesn't have much of an impact in marriage and family life, but being serious about your faith does make a difference.

Why is this? I think it's largely because our understanding of love is more like the world's than like God's. We tend to view love more as a warm and sentimental feeling rather than a deliberate choice or action that exists contrary to feelings. More than we care to admit, we believe that when the sentimental feeling leaves the relationship, the relationship is gone as well. But this isn't love; it's relational consumerism.

Love is the willful commitment we make to others to serve them and place their welfare before our own, even when we don't feel like it. When we say, "I just don't love you anymore," we're really saying, "I just don't feel like investing in you anymore."

Instead of "Do I love this person anymore?" we need to be asking, "Am I *willing* to love this person?" If we are, we have to find a way to do it. If not, we have to examine our own hearts. Love says, "I will continue to serve and love you, even in the absence of those feelings."

It shouldn't be surprising that people who live by the latter value are more likely to end up with happy and fulfilling relationships than those who try to cash in one currently emotionless relationship for another.

Love Has Died Reality

Research shows that unhappy couples who stick it out are far more likely to end up with a happy relationship five years later than people who divorce. In a recent study, 80 percent of unhappy married couples who remained married reported being very happily married five years later, even when intensive marital therapy didn't play a part. These couples just worked through the rough spots and life got better. The same report found that very few unhappy couples who divorced reported life being any happier after the breakup.[8] Hanging in there and making it work is a much more fruitful option; it's more in line with the true nature of love that God created us for.

REALITY OF IT ALL

Of all the places to live as a family, reality may not be the easiest. But it's the best because that's where God is. Satan originally sought to create new realities in our minds by questioning God's wisdom: "Indeed, has God said . . . ?" and "You surely shall not die!" (Genesis 3:1,4). Satan still works to create new realities, and we must always check our understanding of something against God's lordship in creation and His holy Word.

I can imagine Yogi Berra, the baseball great known for his oversimplified statements, saying, "If you're not livin' in reality, you're livin' someplace else."

God's Reality

Live in reality! Seize it and rejoice in it because that's where God lives and works His glorious redemption.

CHAPTER 9

ENEMIES OF A CHRISTIAN FAMILY

*Catch for us the foxes, the little foxes that ruin the
vineyards, our vineyards that are in blossom.*

SONG OF SONGS 2:15, NIV

The kids and I were playing at the park on a Saturday recently.
As we sat under a tree and took a rest, we watched a funny
little drama play out in the world of woodland creatures. Another
family had left a bunch of cheese puffs on the ground where they
had been picnicking. One little squirrel had its eye on the family
and sprung into action as soon as they vacated. It quickly scur-
ried over, gathered a big cheese puff in its mouth—a sight in
itself—and carried it off to the base of a tree. As it went back for
more, a Blue jay swooped down and snatched the squirrel's just-
gathered booty. When the squirrel returned with the next load,
you could almost read its face: "Hey, didn't I just leave a yummy
cheese puff here?" He'd dump the new load, almost seem to shrug
his shoulders, and go back for more. Undetected, the bird would
do its pirate raid again. This continued for a couple of trips. The
poor squirrel thought he was building up a snack-food store for
himself, but he was actually only making life easy for a feathered
pickpocket.

We have to think about the same, less-amusing danger in our
own lives. What are the "little foxes" the Bible talks about that

slyly sneak in and steal the blossom off the vineyard of your family? We know the more obvious vandals: the little aphids of bitterness that plant themselves in our hearts and choke out the joy of our relationships. We know the swarming locusts of infidelity that devour an entire field in moments. The hail of insensitivity that beats down all life in its devastating torrents. The weevil of rebellion in an angry teenage child.

But what about the little foxes that slyly steal into our lives undetected and cause just as much damage to the fruitfulness of our Christian families? As Christ-ones, we need to be alert to these stealthy enemies of the Christian home. Let's start with the most pervasive.

The Fox of Failing to Think Christianly

Harry Blamires, one of C. S. Lewis's students at Oxford, wrote a wonderful book in the early 1960s bemoaning the loss of authentic Christian thinking. He explained that this was especially tragic because "there is nothing in our experience, however trivial, worldly, or even evil, which cannot be thought about Christianly."[1]

Often, we tend to think Christianly about only a few things that relate to morality or strictly religious affairs. We don't think Christianly about many of the things in God's glorious world even though, as George MacDonald recognizes so beautifully, "no place on earth henceforth I shall count strange, for every place belongeth to my Christ."[2] And the deeper essence of family is one of these places. I've tried to provide a fuller picture of that in these pages.

At the risk of being controversial, let me say that while we are to think biblically, I believe that we are to think biblically *and* Christianly. You might ask, "Aren't these the same thing?" While they should be, they aren't always. Let me explain.

The Pharisees thought "biblically" for their day. They observed and obeyed every jot and tittle of the Law. They were fanatics about keeping the Law, but Jesus said they "neglected the weightier provisions of the law" (Matthew 23:23). They missed the whole spirit of God and became His enemies. Like these religious leaders of Jesus' earthly days, it's possible for us to focus on obeying God's Word yet still miss God. This is often true of people who aren't seeking God in the illuminating light of Scripture but are merely focused on drawing attention to their own spirituality. This error is rooted in spiritual pride and arrogance, and it can be a very ugly thing.

One difference between thinking Christianly and thinking "biblically" (in the narrow sense) is that we sometimes mistakenly think we can approach Scripture as a collection of proof-texts that we assemble into a mental concordance. When faced with an issue or question, we search mentally through the list of individual verses we've stored in our heads or we literally search through the concordance in the back of our Bibles to find a verse that we think applies. Problem solved. And if we can't find an applicable passage, we assume God is silent on the issue.

Let me give you a very poignant example from a few decades ago. After the U.S. Supreme Court "discovered" a constitutional right to abortion in 1973, *Christianity Today* ran a number of articles showing how evangelical Christians were divided on the issue. One article quoted a well-known pastor from Dallas, a tireless defender of the truth of God's Word who preached it passionately from his pulpit every week. No liberal to be sure! But when asked for his views on the Court's new decision, he gave this stunning answer, which finds no home in God's Word: "I have always felt that it was only after a child was born and had life separate from its mother that it became an individual person, and it has always, therefore, seemed to me that what is best for the mother and the future should be allowed."[3] Likewise, W. Barry Garrett, Washington bureau chief of Baptist Press extolled the Court's decision with this strange declaration: "Religious liberty, human equality, and justice are advanced by the Supreme Court abortion decision."[4]

These were serious Christians who loved God's Word and sought to live under its guidance. But did they assume that because abortion wasn't mentioned directly in Scripture, God was silent and they should simply adopt the spirit of the day? They might have been thinking "biblically" in a narrow sense, but they weren't thinking Christianly. They missed the spirit of God's creation, that all human life, at every stage, comes to us from God and bears His image, regardless of age and development. How could they fail to appreciate that their beautiful Savior came to us in the form of a preborn child, therefore sanctifying every stage of human life? We know this from thinking biblically in a larger sense.

These leaders could be so far astray because their narrow "proof-texting" failed to help them understand God's Word for what it is: a collective revelation. It's a full revelation of what kind of god God is and what He's doing in the world. We must interpret every verse of Scripture we encounter under the illumination of the rest of the Bible and what it all tells us about the character of

God, His purpose in creation, and how we stand before all of it.

Thinking "biblically" can reduce discipleship to a collection of rules and guidelines. But to think Christianly is to seek the will and purpose of God in the fullness of God's revelation in His holy, infallible Word. This is a subtle but important distinction.

A Christian mind informed by the fullness of God's holy Word understands *all of life* in terms of creation, Fall, Incarnation, and redemption.

Creation: God created everything—*everything*—for His pleasure. He pronounced it good in its original creation. Humanity is the crown of creation because men and women uniquely bear the image of God. Therefore, every person is to be treated with dignity and respect. For family, this means that all of marriage and parenthood is good. Every part of our participation in these things, no matter how small, absolutely fascinates God. Our participation in the life He gave us is a central and unique part of God's revelation of Himself in the world.

Fall: Things didn't stay perfect in God's creation. Satan, one of God's servants, used his God-given free will to challenge rather than serve God. He deceived the first man and woman into distrusting and disobeying God. The consequences of this disobedience were grave, as sin and death entered the world and affected every part of creation. Therefore, things are not as they were. For family, this means relationships between man and woman and their children are not as God meant them to be. They can be difficult sometimes and they can seem impossible. And they will always be less than they could be until the promise of redemption is fully delivered.

Incarnation: In Christ, the God of creation became part of the creation. This is huge! He who was fully God became fully man. Christ's incarnation sanctifies every part of that which is truly human and gives us hope that creation will once again be what it originally was. This means that the whole enterprise of family is deeply sacred because it is here that God became man and lived as man.

Redemption: God is making all things new and all of creation is groaning toward the fullness of what it will someday be again. Christianity is a faith of hope, promise, and renewal. This means God works His redemption through our families and is making each of us into what He always intended us to be. We are to forgive as He forgives and to seek the renewal of those close to us as God does.

These realities should inform everything we learn in Scripture and understand about our place in the world and our place before God. These biblical distinctives *are* the Christian story.

If we don't think Christianly and live out our family life in the fullness of the Christian story, we're living it out in some lesser story. Ask yourself, "How is my understanding and the living out of my Christian family distinctly different from that of my nonChristian, conservative neighbors?" The answer to this question will help you determine how Christian your thinking is in contrast to being simply moral or generically religious. Following Christ in our families is so much more than following some tradition or system.

The Fox of Following the Crowd

George MacDonald said something that might strike many as anything but a Christian ideal: "All wickedness tends to destroy individuality and declining natures assimilate as they sink."[5] We tend to think of individuality as an unchristian ideal. We think of it as going our own way rather than going God's way. But is that necessarily so?

Can individuality actually be godly? Think about cults. They demand strict conformity to a very narrow definition of dress and behavior. Think about the Pharisees who did much the same thing. Think about criminal profiles; there are many common traits among all pedophiles, all rapists, and all serial killers. That's what helps criminal profilers pinpoint what these criminals will do next. Think about Nazism, Communism, and Fascism. None of these tolerated much diversity or individuality.

But it's different in the kingdom of God, which is more tolerant of individuality. Why? Because Christians understand that the Trinitarian God imagined and created us as individuals. The Father loves us as individuals. Christ died for each of us as individuals. And the Spirit calls us and fills us with new life as individuals. We're redeemed as individuals. And God will take us, individually, to Himself when our lives here are done. Revelation 2:17 tells us that, for those who overcome, Christ will call us individually by a special and intimate name that only our Lord and the individual will know. The offering of this special name will be a powerful and intimate declaration that God personally loves and knows us. It will declare to us how uniquely God sees each of us. Individuality figures big in God's economy.

This is why Christ's church through the ages has been the most diverse collection of people gathered around a central purpose than any other people in the world. In 1 Corinthians 12, the apostle Paul teaches that a primary quality of Christ's body is its diversity. Each part of the body serves a particular role. Not everyone is a nose, a mouth, a foot, an arm, or an armpit. Each is called by God to be what he or she was created to be.

We're All Individuals, Everyone

Now you are Christ's body, and individually members of it. . . .
For the body is not one member, but many. (1 Corinthians 12:27,14)

This holds true in a Christian family too. We need to appreciate the individuality of our spouse, children, parents . . . and ourselves. We shouldn't try to be a carbon copy of the family we sit next to in church. We should take the principles God gives us about family life and live them out in our uniqueness.

In the Christian community, we often see movements, books, and conferences that suggest there's only one way (God's way, of course) for doing a number of family tasks: nursing versus bottle feeding, homeschooling versus sending kids to school, feeding a baby on request versus strict scheduling, dating versus courtship. Jackie and I regularly fight this temptation in our own family because of well-meaning friends who are so convinced about some new thing God has led them into. They can make us feel like we should do the same thing—or we'll be missing God. Listen to God regarding the uniqueness of your family. Don't let others try to jam you into their box! If you're following someone else's plan, you could very likely miss God's plan for your family.

The Fox of Lack of Vision and Purpose

Seeking God for what He has for the uniqueness of your family produces a wonderful fruit: intentionality. Families that don't seek direction on where they should be going, what they should be doing, and how they should be doing it drift aimlessly into whatever comes.

But the impact a family can have on its family members *and* on the community where God places it is far too precious to allow it to evolve from whatever might happen. Family is like a grand adventure. You want to have a clue about where you're going and how you're going to get there.

Some experts have encouraged families to draft a family mission statement. While this might make family sound like a cold corporation, I think the spirit of the suggestion is good. Each family should know what its purpose is and how it hopes to accomplish it. The mission should fit the individuality of your family.

Given the talents, passions, and hearts God has given those in your family, ask Him what He wants you to do. This can be very specific or very general. Seek God, talk about it in your family, and ask good friends who know you well, "What should our family be about? What does it seem that God has given us a talent and passion for?"

Crafting a Family Mission Statement

What job do you believe God has for your family to accomplish and how? Make sure it's big enough to convey the vision God has for families but specific enough to allow you to narrow in on accomplishing the mission. Will this mission statement still apply to your family in fifteen years? It should!

We believe God's mission for the _____ *family is:*

The Fox of Sheer Busyness and Stress

This is perhaps one of the most overlooked enemies of the Christian family. While work is good and was a part of the pre-Fall world, Dr. Richard Swenson warns us that we don't leave enough protective space between activities and duties and our rest that leads to a quiet, humane life. He calls this space "margin."

What Does It Mean to Be Marginless?

Dr. Richard Swenson writes,

> Marginless is being thirty minutes late to the doctor's office because you were twenty minutes late getting out

of the hairdresser's because you were ten minutes late dropping off the children at school because the car ran out of gas two blocks from the gas station—and you forgot your purse.

Margin, on the other hand, is having breath left at the top of the staircase, money left at the end of the month, and sanity left at the end of adolescence. . . .

Marginless people are exhausted. Like the mother of four from LaGrange, Illinois, who said: "I'm so tired, my idea of a vacation is a trip to the dentist. I just can't wait to sit in that chair and relax." People are breaking the speed limit of life. Like the man who confessed, "I feel like a minnow in a flash flood."[6]

We often live as if the proverb "Idle hands are the Devil's workshop" is found in Scripture. We ignore the fact that we serve a God who rested and commands us to rest. And we fill our lives with activity. We find ourselves so busy doing all kinds of good things that we don't have time to just simply "be" with others. We are more like busy Martha (Stewart) than Mary, who simply sat with Christ and enjoyed His company (see Luke 10:38-42).

I've had days when I tuck my children into bed, give them a kiss, and realize I haven't talked to them that day. Perhaps we interacted and chatted about all kinds of things since I came home from work, but we didn't *really* talk. We didn't connect. We need to make more time for just being together, doing nothing more than enjoying each other's company. This is where the really good stuff of relationships happens.

The great Christian thinker Blaise Pascal said, "The less [man] were diverted, the happier he would be, like the saints and God. . . . The sole cause of man's unhappiness is that he does not know how to . . . stay at home and enjoy it. Telling man to rest is the same as telling him to live happily."[7]

THE FOX OF "I HAVE TO BE PERFECT"

One of the biggest obstacles that keeps us from being authentic and effective in most things—including family life—is feeling that we need to be perfect. Do you know families that seem to be storybook perfect, like the citizens of Garrison Keillor's mythical Lake Wobegon, "where all the women are strong, all the men are good-looking, and all the children are above-average"? Families like that creep me out. And it's not that I feel good about families that are full of miserable wretches. I just feel much more comfortable with families like my own: a group of fallen people seeking to live out, in tangible ways, Christ's redemptive work in the midst of an honest and human home life. We all screw up and it's best to be honest about it.

Where did we ever get the idea that a good Christian family is a perfect family? Again, we certainly don't find those kinds of families in Scripture. What we do find are graphically human families that are in the process of being slowly pulled into God's redemptive care. Christ's grace and redemption shine in our imperfection (see Romans 5:20).

Comprehending this requires us to understand two important words in the Christian vocabulary: *justification* and *sanctification*.

We're made perfect in God's eyes when we trust in Christ's

death on the cross to cover our sin. That's *justification.* Christ's sacrificial death is the only means by which we can be made right in God's eyes. Along with all other Christians, I'm right in God's eyes, not because of *what* I do or don't do, but because of *who* I trust and love. I don't trust in my own perfection, because only fools trust in things that don't exist! Instead, my imperfection drives me to Christ, who alone is perfect. Trusting in and identifying with Christ is what Christians have always understood as *justification.* And justification is immediate.

Another process in the Christian life is related to justification. This one isn't immediate, but rather is worked out over time. It's called *sanctification.* As we trust in Christ for His righteousness, God's Holy Spirit comes to live within us to help us understand and deal with the sin in our lives. The Holy Spirit meets each one of us just as God created each one of us and Christ died for each one of us: as individuals. And He shows us our sin and imperfection in different ways and on different timetables. Some come to trust Christ and immediately become aware of the sin in their lives—be it pornography, arrogance, dishonesty, or gossip—and God immediately sets them free from it. For others, it takes longer to be free from the physical practice of such sin, and God works with us through the months and years to bring us to a place of God-honoring holiness.

Because sanctification is a process, it looks different and follows a different timeline for each one of us. We should live honestly in the process of sanctification, glorying in the change it brings in our lives, and being hopeful and honest in the change yet to come. Sanctification is about perfection as a destination.

But it's not where any of us currently lives. When we try to appear to be perfect on our own, it's like a fence that keeps out Christ's sanctifying work. When we honestly live out our sanctification, our family members and neighbors get a more vibrant picture of what God's redeeming work looks like. They see and experience how sanctification transforms a less-than-perfect life into something beautiful for Christ's kingdom.

Let's keep all of these foxes from spoiling the fruit of our vineyards by

- thinking (and then acting) biblically *and* Christianly and teaching our children to do so.
- following what God has for us as individuals, not the rest of the crowd. Teaching our children to hear from God for themselves by hearing God for ourselves in front of them.
- loving Christ in our family with vision and purpose, knowing what we want to accomplish for Christ's kingdom in the days He's given us.
- protecting our family from the corrosive effects of busyness and stress. Remembering that rest and leisure are a part of God's cycle of life.
- freeing ourselves from the tyranny of the false idea of perfection and remembering that we're now justified, made right in God's sight by Christ's work, but that our sanctification is in the process of being worked out every day. Let's be honest about that process.

Remembering these things keeps the foxes from the grapes.

CHAPTER 10

WHAT MAKES A CHRISTIAN HOME?

*And the more I considered Christianity, the more I found
that while it had established a rule and order, the chief
aim of that order was to give room for good things to
run wild.*

G. K. CHESTERTON, ORTHODOXY

*The house is only a stage set up by stage carpenters for
the acting of what Mr. W. B. Yeats has called "the drama
of the home." All the most dramatic things happen at
home, from being born to being dead. What a man
thinks about these things is his life: and to substitute
them for the bustle [of public life] is to wander about
among screens and pulleys on the wrong side of paste-
board scenery; and never to act the play. And that play
is always a miracle play; and the name of its hero is
Everyman.*

G. K. CHESTERTON, IRISH IMPRESSIONS

I came to trust Christ in the midst of what was called the Jesus
Movement of the 1970s. I recall a little challenge that went
around in those circles: "If you were arrested for being a
Christian, would there be enough evidence to convict you?" It's a
good question.

But as I've grown in my faith, I've come to realize that it's not
the *amount* of evidence that matters, but the *kind* of evidence. A

zillion Christian bumper stickers on your car or carrying a Bible everywhere you go would get you "convicted" of being a Christian. But these things really say nothing about the substance of your love for Christ.

What if you came to my house for a month and observed the Stanton family's daily routine? What if I came to your house to do the same? What would give either of us a clue that we're observing a Christian family?

I actually think about this a great deal. I think about it in terms of my children. By sheer experience and routine, what are they learning from their home about the essence of Christianity? Would it be that we have Bibles around our house and read from them regularly? Is it that we're part of a local church and involved in the activities there? Would it be that we often listen to worship music in our van and house? These would be good indicators, but are they enough evidence of our family's faith? Should other things be present in our home that would give you an idea of the substance of our faith? We wrestle with these questions. We want to make sure we clearly reveal our Christianity to any observer in our home or of our family. We want to make sure the qualities you'd see in our home are genuinely Christian and substantive. If you've read this far, I'm sure you have the same desire.

As we think about the qualities and distinctives that make a Christian home, it is important to point out from the start that there is no such thing as a Christian home. A home can't be convicted of its sin and cry out to God for mercy and repentance. A home can't profess faith in Christ and seek to love Him. Homes don't become Christians. People do. People live in homes where they have the opportunity to live out their faith in and love for Christ. As they do, their homes become places that reflect the character, redemption, and love of Christ.

This may seem like a quibbling point, but it's important because we don't create a Christian home simply by declaring it one. Our children and neighbors observe and experience our homes as Christian when they see us living in the love and lordship of Christ in our day-to-day domestic lives. In fact, if we're doing this, it won't be necessary to call attention to the fact that our home is a Christian home with plaques on our walls and bumper stickers on our cars. As we live out our lives as Christ-ones in authenticity, our homes will become like a city on a hill that cannot be hidden, radiating for all to see.

A Truly Christian Home Cannot Be Hidden

As we live out our love for and obedience to Christ, our homes will stand out in our communities as beautiful beacons of hope and a challenge toward godliness. Be ready for the response!

"You are the light of the world. A city set on a hill cannot be hidden" (Matthew 5:14).

With that, let's look at the primary qualities that we should expect to see in a home of Christ-ones.

LOVE

The great Christian thinker and evangelist Francis Schaeffer wrote many influential books in an effort to help the church be the church. He came to a point when he knew he was losing a battle with cancer, and he imagined he had enough days left to finish one more book. He knew the last chapter of that book would be the last thing he could say to the world. He wanted it to be important, so he did something interesting.

At the end of his last book, *The Great Evangelical Disaster,* Schaeffer asked his publisher to tack on as the last chapter a short little book he had written and published many years earlier: *The Mark of a Christian.*

What did he say was the mark of a Christian? The same thing Paul said. It is not holiness, service, knowledge, church membership, faith, boldness, or inner strength. *The primary mark of a Christian is love.* Paul explained in 1 Corinthians 13 that if we have all kinds of wonderful spiritual talents and gifts but don't have love, we're less than nothing. In fact, if we have all these things but don't have love, we're ugly and annoying.

The Mark of a Christian

"A new commandment I give to you, that you love one another, even as I have loved you, that you also love one another. By this all men will know that you are My disciples, if you have love for one another." (John 13:34-35)

Think about the two great commandments Christ gave us. In these two, He told us, all the other laws are wrapped:

1. Love God with every part of your being.
2. Love those around you as you love yourself.

Everything else comes after these two things. Scripture tells us, "The one who does not love does not know God, for God is love" (1 John 4:8).

As we've discussed, love isn't an emotion. It's a decision to serve others rather than self. Service to others should be the mark of a Christian home. If we're not interested in love, we can't truly be interested in God, for God *is* love. He's the source of love. He's the originator of it. Love is what He's all about. It's His essence. It must be what we are about.

How does your home rate in its capacity for and desire to love? If investigators were searching your family for evidence of love, would there be enough genuine evidence to convict you?

LORDSHIP

Throughout most of the history of Christianity, the church has developed creeds to help believers understand and remember what they believe and what they don't. Creeds are important to the ongoing life of the church. Many Christians are familiar with the Apostles' Creed and the Nicene Creed. The oldest creed of the Christian church, however, is the simplest as well as the most profound. All the other creeds are footnotes to this one. This creed is just three words long, but it says everything. Early Christians used to greet each other with it, proclaiming, "Jesus is Lord!"

Christians have always recognized that Christ is Lord over every part of creation. Every part of creation holds Christ's intense interest. As Colossians 1:16-17 tells us, Christ created *all* things and He is at every moment holding *all* things together. And verse 20 tells us He is also redeeming *all* things. When I teach on this topic, I always ask the audience, "Think of what is excluded from the category 'all.' Take those things away, place them in a bucket, and those are the things that hold no interest to God!" Of course, there's *nothing* in that bucket because *all* means *all*! Nothing is left out. God created it all. God is fascinated with it all. God is redeeming it all. So, what part of creation is of no interest to Christians? Whatever is in that bucket!

The Extent of Christ's Interests

In John's revelation, he sees the elders fall down before the throne of Christ and proclaim: "Worthy art Thou, our Lord and our God, to receive glory and honor and power; for Thou didst create *all* things, and because of Thy will they existed, and were created" (Revelation 4:11, emphasis added).

Blaise Pascal (1623–1662) responded strongly to Christians who believe that God has little ongoing interest in the world down here: "My God, what stupid arguments! Would God have created the world in order to damn it?"[1]

Dr. Richard Mouw, president of Fuller Theological Seminary, explains in the wonderful little book *He Shines in All That's Fair,*

"As God unfolds his plan for creation, he is interested in more than one thing. Alongside of God's clear concern about the eternal destiny of individuals are his designs for the larger creation."[2] The great Christian reformer John Calvin said that all of creation is at every moment sustained by "the continual rejoicing of God in his work."[3] I like that explanation because it draws such a beautifully true picture of God.

Christ's interest in all of creation flows from His sheer delight in every part of it. Christ-ones should also reflect this interest in every aspect of creation—including family, of course. This is what it means to recognize and live out the church's first creed: Jesus is Lord.

Our homes should be places where we explore the God-endowed glory of human existence and creation—cooking, art, literature, learning, personal grooming, music, humor, friends, hard work, drama, sports, gardening, and more—with relish because we're participating in God's creation and taking delight in all aspects of it, just as He does. And we can find goodness in these things, not as a means toward evangelism or spiritual maturity, but *simply for their own goodness*, recognizing this is exactly why and how God delights in them. They serve no greater end than that they please Him. And we please Him when we enjoy them as He does and recognize them as from Him.

This understanding recognizes the fullness of Christ's lordship over all of creation, not just the religious segments of life. To limit our spiritual interests to only "churchy" areas actually limits Christ's rule. Our spiritual lives should involve all that is of interest to our Lord. Our homes and families should reflect this.

We should teach our children to recognize the glory of God in the fullness of His creation.

If you asked your children right now what God was interested in, what would they say? Their answer demonstrates their understanding of Christ's lordship. Help them develop answers as vast as His lordship.

Supernatural Faith

Just as we're to recognize God's hand and interest in all of nature and human experience, we must also realize God's hand in the supernatural. He works in the world we inhabit and also works in a realm beyond this physical one. One isn't higher or greater than the other, because God created all of it!

We limit our understanding if we fail to live actively in a supernatural realm where evil seeks to pervert creation and humanity and where Christ overcomes Satan, who seeks to do us great harm. We must teach our children to recognize God's hand in both realms. We must have faith that the supernatural realm— which is beyond what we can see—truly exists and that things of real consequence happen there. We need to understand that prayer matters in both the natural and the supernatural realms. We must understand that worship affects us in the natural realm, but also gets things done in the supernatural. In *Eclipse of Heaven*, A. J. Conyers laments that, while Christians may not be naturalists in conviction or belief, we certainly are in practice.[4] We have little real vision and passion for heaven. Too often, our faith doesn't keep us active in the supernatural realm. We *act* as if the natural order of this world is all there is, whether we believe it or not. Do we pray in bold faith for healing, for protection from the destructive designs of Satan's evil schemes, or that a meddlesome coworker who seeks to sandbag our effectiveness will be thwarted by the loving care and goodness of God? Do we boldly believe that God can see a seemingly impossible project through?

We should be naturalists and supernaturalists because God is there and Christ is Lord of both realms. To ignore or belittle either is to be unfaithful to who God is and how and where He works.

What are the tangible signs that your family believes and lives in a universe where supernatural happenings occur that are real and that matter in everyday life?

REDEMPTION

The gospel and kingdom of God are all about redemption: God taking back all that Satan perverted in his failed subversion of God's rule (see Genesis 3:1-5). That includes us and our lives. God's redemption is complete in that Christ made all things right at His crucifixion and resurrection. Remember, the theological word for this is *justification*. But it's still being worked out in the lives of those who trust Christ: the word for that is *sanctification*.

It's essential we live honestly before our loved ones in this process of redemption. This means we need to seriously pursue holiness in God's ongoing redemption, but we must also extend grace to ourselves, our family members, and our friends when we and they blow it.

I find it curious that for a people whose lives are all about redemption, we have very little patience for the process. We try very hard to act as if the whole process has been completed. But we know we all still struggle with sin. We should be honest about this and seek help from God and the community of believers around us. There's nothing wrong and everything good about admitting that we're in process and God is working on us in His way in His time. If you don't believe this, look at the people in the Bible that God used so mightily. Every one of them had major issues, so much so that few of us would have chosen them to do God's work. But God did, and in their flaws shines the grace of God.

Allow your children, spouse, and parents to see you being redeemed. Be appropriately honest about your struggle with specific areas of sin. You don't want to announce to your Bible study group or your children next week that you lust after someone at work, but you should share such honesty with a close friend who can hold you accountable for taking protections against it. Pray for the Holy Spirit to fill you and help you overcome the sin that so easily traps and brings us down. Realize that Christ has secured your salvation on the cross and that your redemption is a process that will conclude one day . . . but not yet. In humility, strive for it, encourage others to strive for it, and give yourself grace when you have setbacks.

Is the process of redemption real in you and your family members' lives, or do you act like it's not possible or that it has already happened? Live in it and let God show Himself through the process.

HOLINESS

The topic of redemption leads us to the topic of holiness. God calls us to be holy as He is holy (see 1 Peter 1:15-16). Holiness is more than making sure our behavior fits within certain boundaries. In *The Problem of Pain*, C. S. Lewis wrote, "The Holiness of God is something more and other than moral perfection: His claim upon us is something more and other than the claim of moral duty." Holiness includes right behavior, to be sure, but it's not confined to behavior. Lewis continues by saying that God is "more than moral goodness: He is not less."[5] Moral goodness is the fruit of the deeper parts of holiness.

So, what is holiness? Few writers have written more truthfully and completely about Christian holiness than J. C. Ryle. He said a person seeking holiness "will strive to be like our Lord Jesus Christ."[6] It's a matter of loving what Christ loves and hating what He hates. God hates ascribing to ourselves or others what belongs to Him. This is why pride is the source of so many other sins. Pride refuses to recognize that all things, even our sufficiency, flow from God. Pride believes, somehow, that God is fortunate to have us. Holiness is something completely different.

Our homes should be fountains flowing with a consuming passion for what God loves. We shouldn't tolerate what He hates. Let's make sure holiness flows from our lives as we seek passionately to love God and see His rule lived out in our lives. True holiness is the natural fruit of such a passion.

How full is your family's pursuit of holiness—loving all that Christ loves and hating what He hates? In what ways does your family have a limited view of holiness? How can it have a more complete view? How would you measure holiness in the life of your family?

Judging "Holiness"

There is a great story of an American Christian magazine writer traveling to England some decades ago to do a story on the Inklings, a celebrated group of Christian writers living near Oxford, England. Among this group were C. S. Lewis, Charles Williams, Warnie Lewis, Owen Barfield, and J. R. R. Tolkien.

The group met on Thursday evenings in Lewis's office and Tuesday mornings at The Eagle and Child pub to enjoy fellowship and share their writing projects with one another. The American reporter wanted a photo to accompany the story. As the members of the Inklings posed around their table in the backroom of the pub, one of the members sensitively asked, "Should we remove our pints and pipes from the table for the sake of the Americans?" Lewis shot back sharply, "No, we should leave our pints and pipes on the table for the sake of the Americans."

Lewis's point is well taken. We tend to measure holiness and godliness by cultural standards and particular outward behaviors. Lewis was telling us it should be judged in deeper places. We must see holiness for what it is: a burning heart for God.

Grace

Our friend Steve, as our mothers might say, is a good Lutheran boy. When he was in college, he got himself arrested for driving while intoxicated. He felt horrible for being so foolish. He had to call his parents from the police station and was afraid his father would hammer him even more than he had hammered himself for his irresponsibility. He explained his situation to his dad and waited for the angry lecture. That's not what Steve got. His dad said instead, "Son, how can I help you through this?" Steve's heart melted.

Steve says this incident is one of the most powerful pictures he ever experienced of God's grace. It was a small picture of the story of the prodigal son and the forgiving father. This kind of grace should mark our homes, for it's a powerful part of the nature of God. Satan condemns and oppresses us. God forgives and offers us freedom. Grace is Satan's most bitter pill, because he wants us condemned.

Think of Christ's story of the prodigal son. Is the spirit of your home more like the gracious heart of the loving father or the hard-hearted, condemning older brother?

Devotion

Devotion should be part of a Christian home. Setting aside regular time to quietly commune with God is essential. Christian writers and preachers often point out that if Christ needed this, we must need it so much more. But that's the wrong way to put it. Christ didn't set time aside with the Father because He needed to. He did it because it's His nature, as a member of the Trinity, to commune with the Father. He was driven by desire. Nothing less should drive us in our devotion.

But what is devotion? Is it a time set aside to pray, read Scripture, and meditate on God, or is it something else? The act of setting aside the time isn't devotion; it's a discipline. Devotion is what the discipline yields: intimacy and communion with God. Devotion isn't an activity but an intimate, personal interaction. The activity yields the communion.

Families should have devotions together. They should have time when they collectively get quiet before God, meditate on some section of Scripture, reflect on some attribute of God, and seek to hear from and talk to Him.[7]

Remember, devotions are a means to an end. The discipline of devotions doesn't matter nearly as much as the opportunity it provides to be close to God. This should be a family affair and a part of every Christian home.

What disciplines does your family practice to foster intimacy with God? What are some that would work for your family, given your spiritual tradition, the age of your children, and the personality of your family?

WORSHIP

Just as we need to seek intimacy with God in devotion, worship is a nonnegotiable part of family life. We should show our children through example that worship isn't just the twenty-minute period of our Sunday morning church service. It's a normal and integral part of everyday Christian life. And it's much more attitude than activity.

The Hebrew word for worship literally means to "bow down." When we worship, we bow down or yield our lives to Christ. Pastor John Piper explains worship as "a way of gladly reflecting back to God the radiance of his worth. It is not a mere act of willpower by which we perform outward acts. . . . Without the engagement of the heart, we do not really worship."[8] Worship must come from every part of our being.

Worship should flow from our hearts throughout the week. This can take place in smaller, more intimate times of worship with family members and friends in a living room or at the table. It can also take place while walking home from school or commuting to work. Worship flows from our hearts and comes from seeing God's hand in unexpected places in our lives and creation — in the natural and the supernatural.

Worship As a Family Affair

Splendor and majesty are before Him, Strength and beauty are in His sanctuary. Ascribe to the Lord, O families of the peoples, Ascribe to the Lord glory and strength. Ascribe to the Lord the glory of His name. (Psalm 96:6-8)

Christian families should make worship a part of both their congregational and their private times with God. Children should learn from their parents — primarily by experiencing it on a regular basis — that vibrant worship is a central part of a believer's everyday life. As a family, explore and experience the various ways believers worship and the kinds of music they use to proclaim and glory in God's wonders and love. Read the Psalms together and learn the various ways and reasons God's people worship Him. Teach your children by direction and example that we can and should worship individually in quiet, simple ways.

What are the ways worship happens in your home? How can you increase the creative ways you and your family members worship as individuals, as a family, and as members of a community?

HOSPITALITY AND SERVICE

James tells us that "pure and undefiled religion in the sight of our God and Father" is to "visit orphans and widows in their distress" (James 1:27). He also tells us that if our faith is not expressed in works of service to others, it is dead (see James 2:17).

Christian homes should be fountains of hospitality and service to our communities. Our children should learn that this flowing forth from ourselves to others is a normal and necessary process in the Christian life. They should learn this is what love does. We should open our homes to others, sharing our food, our resources, and ourselves. We should seek to serve others, just as Christ served His disciples by humbly doing the lowly work of washing their dirty, dusty, stinking feet. We should serve others both in our homes and out where people who need us are.

We can teach our children to be creative in serving and giving to others. They need to learn, not by our words, but by our example. Encourage your children to think of creative ways to meet the needs of others, given their particular passions and talents. Be prepared for the interesting (and perhaps unorthodox) ways your children might want to serve others. I remember as a young teen wanting badly to write letters to prisoners in a penitentiary out in the country near the town where I grew up. It would be my way of visiting them. My parents let me try, but prison chaplains warned it wasn't safe for a boy so young to engage criminals, so I didn't. But thinking about and seeking to do it were good experiences for me.

Love, which is the mark of a Christian, seeks to serve others. Serving others should be a part of a Christian home. Your family is like a pool that the blessings of God flow into. To stay healthy, those blessings must flow out to others. If not, the pool gets stagnant. How is your family flowing out in service and hospitality to others?

JUST THE BASICS

This isn't an exhaustive list of the qualities that mark a Christian home. But they are some of the essentials. We don't all need to do them the same way. Remember, God's kingdom is a place where we can live in the individuality God has given us. While individualism can be a harmful thing when it's selfishly motivated, we should seek God for ourselves and allow a godly individuality in our homes that helps each of us to follow after God and love Him with the passions, talents, and desire He has uniquely placed within us.

God didn't create any of us out of a box, so we shouldn't force each other into one. We must seek to make sure that the evidence that would convict us as Christians is the deeper and more basic stuff that makes up an authentically Christian home.

CHAPTER 11

ENDING WITH THE FIRST THING
FOR CHRISTIAN FAMILIES

*Create in me a clean heart, O God, and put a new and
right spirit within me.*

PSALM 51:10, RSV

*Say the welcoming word to God—"Jesus is my
Master"—embracing, body and soul, God's work of
doing in us what he did in raising Jesus from the dead.
That's it. You're not "doing" anything; you're simply
calling out to God, trusting him to do it for you. That's
salvation. With your whole being you embrace God setting things right, and then you say it right out loud:
"God has set everything right between him and me!"*

ROMANS 10:9-10, MSG

I was raised in a Christian home. Come Sunday morning, we
were either sitting attentively on the front pew at church or
sick in bed at home. Those were the only two options.

The heavy levels of pew time made me quite familiar with all
the details of the Christian story: Creation, the Fall, original sin,
the Ten Commandments, Christ's birth, life, death, and resurrection, and the beginning of the Christian movement. The Apostles'
Creed was emblazoned on my mind from relentless repetition. I
knew the main points of the story, but I didn't know the story. No

one had ever explained to me how it all fit together into a whole. This left me drifting and confused in many ways.

Then, in my seventeenth year of life, I met a remarkable auburn-haired girl who dramatically altered the shape and direction of my life in ways deeper than I could ever imagine. Among the most dramatic of these alterations was helping me put all the parts of the story together into a story, *the* story.

This story served as the foundation of growth for every part of my life, including my family that was to come. This story is also the foundation of your life (whether you realize it or not), because it's the foundation of all reality. Let me share with you what that wonderful messenger told me.

One afternoon after school, we were in the foyer of her mom's home, sitting on the floor, talking. I don't remember how we got on the subject, but she started telling me about God's story. Maybe she sensed I didn't have much of a clue.

She told me that God wanted to share His love and intimacy with a larger group than the community of the Trinity. For sheer desire and delight, God created a wonderful world, placed the first two humans in the midst of it, and gave them the gift of knowing and loving God, loving each other, participating in the gift of bringing forth new life, and caring for His creation. That's what we had at the dawn of creation, in the garden. It was perfect.

But God couldn't make us love Him, as love must be given freely. For love to be love, we must choose to love. But God also knows that the opportunity to choose love is also the same opportunity to choose something else.

Satan, God's created servant-turned-enemy (because he chose

himself, rather than love), persuaded Adam and Eve—our first parents—to use their free will to break their perfect relationship with God by disobeying Him. That changed everything and set it all wrong for everyone who would come forth from Adam and Eve. That is what Christians have always understood as "original sin," and it keeps all of us from experiencing the relationship and intimacy with God we were created for. It also dramatically affected the relationship between Adam and Eve as well as their own internal relationships with themselves. With this primary relationship with God severed, we'll seek to satisfy that still-present need for completion and relationship in places other than God. We'll always seek what we were made for; but because our relationship with God is broken, it leaves us looking in all kinds of wrong places.

This is the source of our practical sin—the sins each of us commits individually on a daily basis. The root of these sins is seeking life and fulfillment in things without recognizing God's proper place. Sin is failing to love God and others as ourselves as God intended, and instead, trying to make life work on our own. Sin is failing to recognize and live in God's lordship over all of life. This failure can take all sorts of forms, from pride and arrogance to false religion, sexual sin, substance abuse, backbiting, gossip, greed, and so on.

So sin separates us from what God created us for: intimacy with Himself and others. God is perfect, holy, and pure and can have no part of sin, so we can't have any part of Him in our present state. This high school girl explained the true dilemma of humanity, something most of the world's greatest philosophers fail to understand: If we can't be whole apart from what we were created for, how can we overcome this chasm that separates us from what we were intended for? This is *the* question. How can we be whole?

It can't be our good deeds, because Scripture tells us that, compared to God's holiness, our good deeds are like filthy, nasty rags (see Isaiah 64:6). Something else must span this chasm between God and humanity. There is a need for one who has the purity of God, but who also struggled in human flesh. That one is Christ, who was mystically just as much God as He was human. He was fully human, but also fully God, without sin. Christ is the bridge over the chasm. In His horrible death on a real cross on a real day some two thousand years ago, He took all the sin of the world upon Himself as if it were His own, and He satisfied the debt we all owe to God for our sins. Only He could do it because He is perfectly God. Only He could do it because He was flesh. The Prince of Peace brought peace between God and humanity.

As Jackie told me these things, it was as if floodlights came on. All the parts of the story fit together and made sense. They all came to a point—a real, meaningful point. I remember clearly the first thing that hit me was understanding why, as Christ was on the cross, the sky turned dark and Jesus asked the Father why He'd left Him there all alone. God couldn't stand to see the sins of the world upon the body of His perfect and beloved Son. Your sins and mine, all of them! Christ took them upon Himself and paid the price to satisfy the debt we created, a debt too great for any of us to pay.

Who Drove Those Nails?

The Dutch painter Rembrandt painted a curious painting in 1633 titled *Raising of the Cross*. As in many of his paintings, the central subject is bathed in light against a background of darkness. The subject in this painting is Christ being raised on the cross, yet something about the painting strikes the viewer as odd.

Those participating in executing Christ are dressed in the garb of the day and society Rembrandt lived in. The painter portrays himself in the painting participating in raising the cross. You might ask, "Hey, what are those seventeenth-century Dutch guys with funky hats doing crucifying Christ?"

But that's exactly the point. Rembrandt was communicating that *he* nailed Christ to the cross, that it was *his* sin that drove Christ there.[1] It could easily be me in the painting and it could easily be you because our sin drove Christ to the cross as well. (To see *Raising of the Cross,* visit www.artchive.com/artchive/R/rembrandt/rembrandt_raising_of_the_cross.jpg.html)

But, as Jackie explained, that wasn't the end. There was Sunday morning: the Resurrection. Christ rose from the dead, conquering sin and death, setting all creation free. Because Christ overcame the sin of the world in His death and resurrection, new life is made available to all of us, as the Scriptures declare.

She brought the story to a close on the whole point of history. The most consequential question each of us must face is this: "What will we do with Christ?"

She asked, "Will we realize our separateness from God and our inability to make the relationship right? Or do we foolishly assume that we're not so far from God?" Do we trust in our own inadequate goodness or in the unique sufficiency of Christ's righteousness, which by His limitless grace He extends to everyone? We must simply recognize our poverty and trust in His singular ability to set us right with God.

But how do we trust? What does this look like? We do this by doing what we sing in a very beautiful but simple song at Christmas: "O come let us adore Him, Christ the Lord." Christians should sing this with their lives every day. For this is the whole end of the Christian life, to adore Christ. And there was never a person who got off track with God because he or she adored Christ too much.

Getting the Balance Right

Blaise Pascal wrote, "Knowing God without knowing our own wretchedness makes for pride. Knowing our own wretchedness without knowing God makes for despair. Knowing Jesus Christ strikes the balance because he shows us both God and our own wretchedness."[2]

Let me capture all this in a nutshell, as if something so grand *can* be captured in a nutshell!

- *There's purpose to life:* intimacy with God and all that is His (that is, creation and others).

- *There's also a dilemma:* our freedom, which love requires, allows us to choose something other than God. That choice has the real consequence of separating us from the purpose of life. And it's our fault, not God's.

- *There's an answer:* Christ, the God-man, by His grace and righteousness, and through His incarnation, death and resurrection, bridges the chasm between humanity and God and brings the two together as God desires them to be.

- *There's a choice:* Will we trust in this truth, which is the only way? (See John 14:6.) Or will we believe we can try to make it work another way? Or will we foolishly do nothing and believe everything is fine as it is?

The pieces came together for me in a way they never had. These were no longer disconnected facts, but a story—a grand and glorious story. I came to learn that this is *the* story from which every other story is but a chapter. It's the golden thread in the narrative that moves through everything.

I took that story to be the narrative of my life, a new life in Christ. And that wonderful girl became my wife in a few years, and together we partnered with God in bringing forth a van-load of little kids in the short span of a few years—but not before years of heart-wrenching infertility. Jackie and I have grown together as a couple, together as parents, and together as followers of Christ, seeking to see His new life made real in our lives and in our children's.

As I confessed to you at the beginning of and throughout this book, we haven't done this perfectly. No one does. We've seen successes, to be sure; God has done remarkable things to help us to reflect the character of His Son. But we've also seen failures—brilliant failures. We blow it regularly. We seek God's forgiveness and He gives it. We press on and thank God for all of it.

That's why I end the book here—at the beginning. This is the most important part. It sets everything else in motion. We must understand where we stand with God without Christ: separated forever from what we were created for, without hope. Only as we see this can we realize what we have through Christ: peace with God and a relationship that makes us new creations.

What's Your Problem?

What's the primary problem with each of us? Why are we so messed up?

For a clue, look at the parables of Jesus on the prodigal son, the lost coin, and the missing sheep. Jesus was telling us that the primary problem between God and humanity isn't a lack of commitment, bad behavior, wrong theology, or (insert your own personal hang-up here). It is something more basic.

As Leighton Ford explains, the religious leaders of Jesus' day "didn't know what sin really is. They thought of sin as badness. But in these stories, Jesus demonstrates that sin is actually *away-ness*. The sheep, the coin, the son were all away from those who treasured them."[3]

And that "awayness" is the source for everything else being

wrong. It's foolish to try to solve any other problem without solving that one. And only Christ can bring us to God.

The Christian family lives this out in real and honest ways and seeks to pass it on faithfully in all its beauty and wonder to the next generation.

GRACE: CONNECTING THE IDEAL WITH THE REAL

The Christian family lives in the time between, which theologians call "the already and the not yet." This is the stretch of time between the sacrificial death of Christ, making us right with Him (the already), and the process of our becoming new creations as well as the full establishment of His kingdom (the not yet). The promise of God's redemptive work keeps us hopeful just as the reality of this present world keeps us humble.

When we accept the story, Christ justifies us and makes us right with the Father. But we're not yet made perfect, and every new day brings evidence of that fact. It's against this reality that we understand *grace*: God's, others' to us, and ours to others. Grace is the mechanism God uses to bring us from where we are to where we will be. Our screw-ups and the "realness" of life are precious tools in God's plan, because they serve to remind us where we came from, that this isn't how life is supposed to be, and that this isn't how it will remain.

This is what Anne Lamott understands in God's pursuit of her in the midst of her family life:

I don't know why life isn't constructed to be seamless and safe, why we make such glaring mistakes, things fall so short of our expectations, and our hearts get broken and our kids do scary things and our parents get old and don't always remember to put their pants on before they go out for a stroll. I don't know why it's not more like it is in the movies, why things don't come out neatly and lessons can't be learned when you're in the mood for them, why love and grace often come in such motley packaging. But I was reminded of the lines of D. H. Lawrence that are taped to the wall of my office:

> What is the knocking?
> What is the knocking at the door in the night?
> It is somebody who wants to do us harm.
> No, no, it is the three strange angels.
> Admit them, admit them.

> . . . I understand that failure is surely one of those strange angels.[4]

Failure is the canvas upon which the beautiful picture of Christ's redemption is brought forth in our lives and the world, stroke by gloriously slow and sure stroke. Family life is guaranteed to have failures because it's such a complicated, complex, and consequential proposition.

Sure, the process of family can be messy. This messiness is much of its virtue. And because God is in it, it's going somewhere, and where it's going is beautiful. That means that no matter how big the mess, the process is also beautiful.

Here, in every aspect of family life, between the already and the not yet—live in it all. Glory in it all because God does.

Seize it. For it's far bigger than you can imagine.

PUTTING IT ALL TOGETHER

*When we defend the family, we do not mean it is always
a peaceful family; when we defend the thesis of marriage, we do not mean it is always a happy marriage.
We mean that it is the theatre of spiritual drama, the
place where things happen, especially the things that
matter.*

G. K. CHESTERTON, THE HOME OF THE UNITIES

How do you love Christ in your family?

The answer to this question is what brought both of us to these
pages, me to write them and you to read them. In this pursuit, we've
explored a lot of things about understanding the nature and drama of
family life in light of the Christian story. You might have been familiar with some of it. Some of it might be new. I pray it was all helpful.

There have been some big themes presented in this book, and
there's nothing more practical than big ideas because they open
up new areas for you to live in. Your understanding of these big
themes is the first step in loving Christ authentically in your family. From here you can seek to live out the particulars in your family. These big themes are:

- Every part of family life, from the glory of childbirth
  to the drudgery of cleaning toilets, is sacred because

God created it all, was born into it, and participated in it in the person of Jesus Christ. This gives us great hopefulness in the midst of it all.

- The union of man, woman, and their children is a living image of the Trinity on earth. This shows us that every family is far more than appearances present.

- Christ created us as individuals, He desires to commune with us as individuals, and that drove Him to die for us as individuals. He calls us to Himself as individuals, redeems us as individuals, and is making us into new creations as individuals. One day, we'll stand before Him as individuals and He'll call those who love Him by a name that only He knows (see Revelation 2:17). This is intimacy; living in this God-given individuality honors God and gives vibrancy to His kingdom in the world.

- The Christian faith has a very high view of human sexuality and the sexual embrace. It's a gift of God, mystically reflecting something of His nature, and it allows us the opportunity to give deeply of ourselves physically, emotionally, spiritually, and creatively to another person. Therefore, sexuality should be confined to marriage, a relationship that promises total commitment and the complete giving of ourselves exclusively. Properly understood, sex is total self-giving; to use another person as a sexual object is the opposite of this ideal. It dishonors all involved, including God.

- Marriage is a unique earthly picture of the relationship of Christ with His church. For this reason, as well as the fact that our spouse is our own flesh, we are to honor our marriage. We honor our marriage by honoring our spouse, giving our complete troth: our faithfulness and fidelity. Right after God, and because of Him, we give our spouse the highest place of honor in our lives. She or he comes first. And this isn't based on feelings, but is in fulfillment of the promise we made on our wedding day. The soil of our spouse's heart will flourish under such honor. And God is pleased.

- When we parent, we reflect the nature of God, who reveals Himself to us as Father. We also experience and demonstrate motherlike qualities of God as life-giver, protector, and nurturer. We're to replicate our Christian faith in our children, helping them become everything God has created them to be. This requires God-directed intentionality.

- As children, we reflect the nature of Christ, who is Someone's Child. We're to obey and honor parents, because this is the relationship Christ had with His heavenly Father as well as His earthly parents. We don't serve a God who can't understand and help with the trials of parenthood and childhood.

- The Christian life is all about us being transformed so that we reflect the image and nature of Christ in the world. God gives His unbounded grace when we blow it, repent, and seek His forgiveness. Therefore, we should extend that same grace to our family members and friends when they blow it with us. Christianity is about grace and transformation.

- The sum of the Christian life is found in loving God with every part of our being and loving others as ourselves. This will be the fruit of those who adore Christ and have surrendered themselves to His rule.

Recognizing these things, reflecting on them often, living them out in the honesty of our lives, and teaching them to our loved ones is how we honor and love Christ authentically in our families.

The intersection of our Christian faith and our family life is an utterly profound thing.

Live in it. Wrestle with it. Seize it. Glory in every last bit of it.

I pray God's peace, love, and grace upon you as you do.

NOTES

INTRODUCTION

1. Alvaro de Silva, ed., *Brave New Family: G. K. Chesterton on Men and Women, Children, Sex, Divorce, Marriage and the Family* (San Francisco: Ignatius Press, 1990), pp. 13, 14, 16.

CHAPTER 1: *Loving Christ in Your Family*

1. Frederick Buechner, *Now & Then* (San Francisco: Harper & Row, 1983), p. 3.
2. C. S. Lewis, *Letters to an American Lady* (Grand Rapids, Mich.: Eerdmans, 1967), p. 44.
3. Dallas Willard, *The Divine Conspiracy: Rediscovering Our Hidden Life in God* (New York: HarperSanFrancisco, 1998), p. 41.
4. Willard, p. 41.
5. Willard, p. 41, emphasis added.
6. Stephen Neill, *The Difference in Being a Christian* (New York: Association Press, 1955), pp. 6, 11, cited in Willard, *The Divine Conspiracy*, p. 42.
7. Gordon T. Smith, *On the Way: A Guide to Christian Spirituality* (Colorado Springs: NavPress, 2001), pp. 26-27.
8. G. K. Chesterton, "On Certain Modern Writers and the Institution of the Family," in *The Collected Works of G. K. Chesterton*, vol. 1, *Heretics, Orthodoxy, The Blatchford Controversies* (San Francisco: Ignatius Press, 1986), n.p., emphasis added.
9. Dietrich Bonhoeffer, *Letters and Papers from Prison* (New York: Macmillan, 1953), letter dated 3 August 1944.
10. Cited in Barry Morrow, *Heaven Observed: Glimpses of Transcendence in Everyday Life* (Colorado Springs: NavPress, 2001), p. 165.

11. Eugene Peterson, *Like Dew Your Youth: Growing Up with Your Teenager* (Grand Rapids, Mich.: Eerdmans, 1998), p. 5.

CHAPTER 2: *Why Do We Hurt the Ones We Love?*

1. Pope John Paul II, *The Role of the Christian Family in the Modern World: Familiaris Consortio* (Boston: Pauline Books & Media, 1981), p. 38.
2. Charles H. Spurgeon, *Treasury of David*, Psalm 101, vol. 2, www.bibleclassics.com
3. Rose M. Kreider and Jason M. Fields, *Number, Timing, and Duration of Marriages and Divorces: 1996*, Current Population Reports, P70-80, U.S. Census Bureau, Washington D.C., February 2002, p. 7.
4. E. Mavis Hetherington, *For Better or For Worse: Divorce Reconsidered* (New York: Norton, 2002), p. 6.
5. Linda J. Waite, et al., *Does Divorce Make People Happy?: Findings from a Study of Unhappy Marriages* (New York: Institute for American Values, 2002), p. 6.
6. Anne Lamott, *Traveling Mercies: Some Thoughts on Faith* (New York: Pantheon Books, 1999), pp. 214-215. Used by permission of the publisher.
7. Gordon T. Smith, *On the Way: A Guide to Christian Spirituality* (Colorado Springs: NavPress, 2001), p. 58.

CHAPTER 3: *What Does a Christian Care About Family Anyway?*

1. Francis A. Schaeffer, *Genesis in Space and Time: The Flow of Biblical History* (Downers Grove, Ill.: InterVarsity, 1972), p. 9.
2. Pope John Paul II, *The Role of the Christian Family in the Modern World, Familiaris Consortio* (Boston: Pauline Books & Media, 1981), sec. 17.
3. Henri J. M. Nouwen, *The Return of the Prodigal Son: A Story of Homecoming* (New York: Image Books, 1994), pp. 134, 137.
4. C. S. Lewis, *Miracles: A Preliminary Study* (New York: Collier Books, 1960), p. 108.
5. For review and summary of this body of literature, see Glenn T. Stanton, *Why Marriage Matters: Reason to Believe in Marriage in Postmodern Society* (Colorado Springs: Piñon Press, 1997).

CHAPTER 4: *Sex: Where It All Starts*

1. Wendell Berry, *Sex, Economy, Freedom, and Community* (New York: Pantheon Books, 1993), pp. 143-144.

2. G. K. Chesterton, "The Cockneys and Their Jokes," in *All Things Considered* (London: Sheed and Ward, 1908), p. 11.

3. Bruce Marshall, *The World, The Flesh and Father Smith* (Boston: Houghton Mifflin, 1945), p. 108.

4. G. K. Chesterton, *G. K.'s Weekly*, 29 January 1927.

5. C. S. Lewis, *Mere Christianity* (New York: Macmillan, 1960), p. 96.

6. Cited in C. S. Lewis, *George MacDonald: An Anthology—365 Readings* (New York: HarperSanFrancisco, 2001), p. 28, emphasis added. From George MacDonald, *Unspoken Sermons,* 1867.

7. Lewis, *Mere Christianity,* p. 65.

8. Lewis, *Mere Christianity,* p. 91.

9. Berry, pp. 138-139.

10. George Weigel, *The Truth of Catholicism: Ten Controversies Explored* (New York: Cliff Street Books, 2001), pp. 104-105.

11. God is the only One for whom it is permissible, and even necessary, to be self-absorbed because He is the proper focus of the whole universe. But because the Christian God exists in Trinity He is not narcissistic. While He is self-focused, each member is focused on the other members, marking a God who simultaneously reflects both a proper self-centeredness and an other-centeredness.

12. Bob Dylan, "Lonesome Day Blues," from *Love and Theft,* Columbia Records, 2001.

13. Lewis, *Mere Christianity,* p. 96.

14. Karl Barth, *Church Dogmatics,* vol. 3/4 (Edinburgh: T & T Clark, 1961), p. 133.

15. Berry, p. 140.

16. Glenn T. Stanton, *Why Marriage Matters: Reasons to Believe in Marriage in Postmodern Society* (Colorado Springs: Piñon Press, 1997), chap. 1; Robert T. Michael, et al., *Sex in America: A Definitive Survey* (Boston: Little, Brown, 1994), p. 131; Edward O. Laumann, et al., *The Social Organization of Sexuality: Sexual Practices in the United States* (Chicago: University of Chicago Press, 1994), p. 364, table 10.5; Linda

Waite and Maggie Gallagher, *The Case for Marriage* (New York: Doubleday, 2000).

17. Michael D. Resnick, et al., "Protecting Adolescents from Harm: Findings from the National Longitudinal Study on Adolescent Health," *The Journal of the American Medical Association* 278 (1997), pp. 823-832.

18. Sharon D. White and Richard R. DeBlassie, "Adolescent Sexual Behavior," *Adolescence* 27 (1992), pp. 183-191.

19. Pope John Paul II, *The Truth and Meaning of Human Sexuality: Guidelines for Education Within the Family* (Boston: Pauline Books & Media, 1996), p. 20.

CHAPTER 5: *Being Someone's Spouse*

1. Karol Wojtyla, *The Jeweler's Shop: A Meditation on the Sacrament of Matrimony, Passing on Occasion into a Drama* (San Francisco: Ignatius Press, 1992), pp. 37, 39. Originally published in the Polish magazine *Znak* in Krakow, December 1960. Used by permission of The Libreria Editrice Vaticana in Rome.

2. Wojtyla, pp. 88-89.

3. Erich Fromm, *The Art of Loving: An Enquiry into the Nature of Love* (New York: Harper & Row, 1956), p. 55-56.

4. Wendell Berry, *Sex, Economy, Freedom & Community: Eight Essays* (New York: Pantheon Books, 1993), p. 139.

5. James H. Olthuis, *I Pledge You My Troth: A Christian View of Marriage, Family, Friendship* (San Francisco: Harper & Row, 1975), p. 22.

6. Wojtyla, p. 26.

7. *The Book of Common Prayer* (1789; reprint, New York: Oxford University Press, 1990), p. 427.

8. G. K. Chesterton, *Fancies versus Fads* (London: Methuen & Co, 1923), p. 197.

CHAPTER 6: *Being Someone's Parent*

1. Cited in C. S. Lewis, *George MacDonald: An Anthology — 365 Readings* (New York: HarperSanFrancisco, 2001), p. 136.

2. George MacDonald, *A Book of Strife in the Form of The Diary of An Old Soul*, 1880, reading for 10 July. Cited at www.ibiblio.org/gutenberg/etext99/doaos10.text

3. Irenaeus, *Against the Heretics* 4.20.7.

4. Elizabeth Barrett Browning, *Aurora Leigh*, bk. 7, lines 821-825, http://www.classicreader.com/read.php/sid.4/bookid.1115/sec.7/ [23 April 2002].

5. Abraham Kuyper, "Sphere Sovereignty," in James D. Bratt, ed., *Abraham Kuyper: A Centennial Reader* (Grand Rapids, Mich.: Eerdmans, 1998), p. 488.

6. Michael D. Resnick, et al., "Protecting Adolescents from Harm: Findings from the National Longitudinal Study on Adolescent Health," *The Journal of the American Medical Association* 278 (1997), pp. 823-832.

7. A copy of this important essay can be found at http://www.uoregon.edu/~dluebke/Reformations441/LutherMarriage.htm [23 April 2003].

CHAPTER 7: *Being Someone's Child*

1. C. S. Lewis, *George MacDonald: An Anthology* (New York: HarperSanFrancisco, 2001), p. xxiii.

2. C. S. Lewis, *The Four Loves* (New York: Harcourt Brace Jovanovich, 1960), p. 13.

3. Blaise Pascal, *Pensées* (New York: Penguin, 1966), no. 377.

4. Dietrich Bonhoeffer, *Life Together* (New York: Harper & Row, 1954), p. 20.

CHAPTER 8: *Myths of a Christian Family*

1. G. K. Chesterton, "The Surprise", in *Collected Works of G. K. Chesterton*, vol. 2 (San Francisco: Ignatius Press, 1989), n.p.

2. Quoted in Dana Mack and David Blankenhorn, *The Book of Marriage: The Wisest Answers to the Toughest Questions* (Grand Rapids, Mich.: Eerdmans, 2001), p. 131.

3. Quoted in Alvaro de Silva, ed., *Brave New Family: G. K. Chesterton on Men and Women, Children, Sex, Divorce, Marriage and the Family* (San Francisco: Ignatius Press, 1990), p. 23.

4. Quoted in Mack and Blankenhorn, p. 401.

5. Quoted in Joseph E. Kerns, "For Better, for Worse," in *The Theology of Marriage* (London: Sheed & Ward, 1964), chap. 11.

6. "Christians Are More Likely to Experience Divorce Than Are

Non-Christians," a report of the Barna Research Group, Ventura, Calif., 21 Dec. 1999, p.2.

7. Larry L. Bumpass, "Family-related Attitudes, Couple Relationships, and Union Stability" in Ron Lesthaeghe, ed., *Meaning and Choice: Value Orientations and Life Cycle Decisions* (The Hague, Netherlands: Netherlands Interdisciplinary Demographic Institute, 2001), p. 168. From the presentation, "Religion and Divorce," Ties that Bind: Religion & Family in Contemporary America, Center for Religious Study, Princeton, N.J., 16 May 2001.

8. Linda J. Waite, et al., *Does Divorce Make People Happy? Finding from a Study of Unhappy Marriages* (New York: Institute for American Values, 2002), p. 5.

CHAPTER 9: *Enemies of a Christian Family*

1. Harry Blamires, *The Christian Mind: How Should a Christian Think?* (1963; reprint, Ann Arbor: Servant Books, 1978), p. 45.

2. George MacDonald, *A Book of Strife in the Form of The Diary of An Old Soul*, 1880, reading for 28 October. Cited at www.ibiblio.org/gutenberg/etext99/doaos10.text

3. "Abortion Decision: A Death Blow?" *Christianity Today*, 16 February 1973, p. 48.

4. "What Price Abortion?" *Christianity Today*, 2 March 1973, p. 39.

5. George MacDonald, *Alec Forbes of Howglen*, 1865, vol. 3, chap. 4, cited in C. S. Lewis, *George MacDonald: An Anthology: 365 Readings* (New York: HarperCollins, 2001), p. 127.

6. Richard A. Swenson, M.D., *The Overload Syndrome: Learning to Live Within Your Limits* (Colorado Springs: NavPress, 1998), pp. 13, 11.

7. Blaise Pascal, *Pensées* (New York: Penguin Books, 1966), nos. 132, 136.

CHAPTER 10: *What Makes a Christian Home?*

1. Blaise Pascal, *Pensées* (New York: Penguin Books, 1966), no. 896.

2. Richard J. Mouw, *He Shines in All That's Fair: Culture and Common Grace* (Grand Rapids, Mich.: Eerdmans, 2001), p. 50.

3. Cited in Susan Schreiner, *The Theater of His Glory: Nature and*

the Natural Order in the Thought of John Calvin (Grand Rapids, Mich.: Baker, 1991), p. 28.

4. A. J. Conyers, *Eclipse of Heaven: The Loss of Transcendence and Its Effect on Modern Life* (South Bend, Ind.: St. Augustine's Press, 1999), especially chaps. 1-2.

5. C. S. Lewis, *The Problem of Pain* (New York: Macmillan, 1944), p. 53.

6. J. C. Ryle, "Holiness: A Sermon," www.iclnet.org/pub/resources/text/history/spurgeon/web/ryle.holiness.html

7. A good book that is helpful in developing a rich devotional time is one I mentioned earlier in this book: Gordon T. Smith's *On the Way: A Guide to Christian Spirituality* (NavPress, 2001). Smith has a few appendices at the back of his book that offer thoughtful advice and rich resources for developing and experiencing an intimate devotional time that is rooted in under-appreciated but time-tested traditions of the church.

8. John Piper, *Desiring God: Meditations of a Christian Hedonist* (Sisters, Ore.: Multnomah, 1996), p. 81.

CHAPTER 11: *Ending with the First Thing for Christian Families*

1. Mariel Westermann, *Rembrandt* (London: Phaidon Press, 2000), pp. 106-107.

2. Blaise Pascal, *Pensées* (New York: Penguin Books, 1966), no. 192.

3. Leighton Ford, *The Power of Story* (Colorado Springs: NavPress, 1994), p. 81.

4. Anne Lamott, *Traveling Mercies: Some Thoughts on Faith* (New York: Pantheon Books, 1999), pp. 143-144. Used by permission.

About the Author

GLENN T. STANTON is a husband, father, writer, and speaker. He and his wife, Jackie, are raising their five small children in Colorado Springs, and they love it. Their life is marked by little sleep, but much joy! Glenn works as Director of Social Research and Cultural Affairs as well as the Senior Research Analyst for Marriage and Sexuality at Focus on the Family. He also serves as a consultant to the Bush administration on getting fathers involved in their children's early literacy development.

He is the author of *Why Marriage Matters: Reasons to Believe in Marriage in Postmodern Society* (Piñon Press, 1997), and is a contributor to two other books: *The Fatherhood Movement: A Call to Action* (Lexington Books, 1999) and *The Little Big Book for Dads* (Welcome, 2001).

Glenn has published articles and reviews in many magazines and journals and is a winner of the 2001 Amy Foundation Writing Award.

Glenn earned a master's degree in Interdisciplinary Humanities with an emphasis in philosophy, history, and religion from the University of West Florida—he couldn't make up his mind about what he wanted to do in life and all of these seemed so fascinating. He has also taught in each of these disciplines.

His favorite things to do are reading nearly anything, writing, playing with his children, simply *being* with his wife, studying art history, and riding his mountain bike really fast down very steep and bumpy mountain trails.

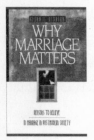